D0350687

Crucial Conversations

Books by May Sarton

POETRY

Encounter in April
Inner Landscape
The Lion and the Rose
The Land of Silence
In Time Like Air
Cloud, Stone, Sun, Vine
A Private Mythology
As Does New Hampshire
A Grain of Mustard Seed
A Durable Fire
Collected Poems, 1930–1973

NOVELS

The Single Hound
The Bridge of Years
Shadow of a Man
A Shower of Summer Days
Faithful Are the Wounds
The Birth of a Grandfather
The Fur Person
The Small Room
Joanna and Ulysses
Mrs. Stevens Hears the Mermaids Singing
Miss Pickthorn and Mr. Hare
The Poet and the Donkey
Kinds of Love
As We Are Now
Crucial Conversations

NONFICTION

I Knew a Phoenix
Plant Dreaming Deep
Journal of a Solitude

Crucial Conversations

A NOVEL BY

MAY SARTON

W · W · NORTON & COMPANY · INC · *New York*

First Edition

Library of Congress Cataloging in Publication Data

Sarton, May, 1912–
Crucial conversations.
I. Title.
PZ3.S249Cr [PS3537.A832] 813'.5'2 74-32232
ISBN 0-393-08725-5

Published simultaneously in Canada
by George J. McLeod Limited, Toronto

Printed in the United States of America

2 3 4 5 6 7 8 9 0

Characters

Reed Whitelaw, 50
Poppy Whitelaw, 50 (formerly Stoddard)
Harry, 22 } their elder children, twins
Susie, 22 }
Emerson, 18, their younger child
Philip Somersworth, 50, their intimate friend
Evelyn Stoddard, 76, Poppy's mother
Cecilia Whitelaw, 78, Reed's mother
Kathy Flanagan, 48, Philip's mistress

Crucial Conversations

Chapter I

The September morning was so fine that Philip decided to walk the half mile to the Whitelaws for their ritual game of tennis and Sunday dinner. He was smiling in anticipation as he took his racquet down and was still smiling as he caught himself in the hall mirror, reassured to note that this tall thin presence in shorts looked a lot younger than fifty. "Not bad, old man, not bad at all," he said to himself and to Perseus, the black cat, who was waiting at the door to be let out. "Come along then!"

He was really quite disgustingly happy this morning, the best kind of happiness that settles in for no reason on an autumn day. Am I becoming smug, he wondered, as he stood outside on the stoop for a moment, watching the poplar leaves, thin gold discs, slip down almost as weightless as the bright air? Not smug, he dared to hope, but lately there had been a certain absence of tension in his life, as though everything had fallen into place to be quietly enjoyed for its own sake, his work included.

At the moment he was engaged in the kind of job he liked, where the challenge was to design something livable and beautiful for little money, a barnlike studio and living quarters for a young man. Poppy would say he did not impose his own ideas, too willing to compromise, but she had never really accepted the particular pleasure it was for Philip to create the right environment for a client, at the expense often of an original design. She was so uncompromising herself!

At that moment Philip nearly stumbled on Perseus "Look out, you silly!" The stumble jarred his poise, and as he reached the gate, he had to admit that he was a little anxious about Poppy. She had seemed more on edge than usual lately and Philip wondered whether she were not in for a bout of colitis. Should he take it on himself to suggest that she see a doctor?

Oh well, he told himself, clicking the gate shut so Perseus could not escape, he would know soon enough and worrying would not help. Poppy's moods and illnesses were the dark side of her glittering charm. By the time he reached the Whitelaws the mercurial creature might well be in soaring spirits.

She was working, she had told him, and that was a good sign, but if only she could take the sculpture a little less seriously! She blazed away for a time and then quite suddenly there was a short-circuit. She lost control, or became ill . . . and she herself did not know why. It was puzzling. And of course her black moods made Reed irritable, he who never felt better than when he was up against challenge.

Philip walked fast, propelled by these ruminations, then forced himself to slow down, and to take it easy.

Why allow anxiety to interrupt the full sweep of the day, the brilliant gold of a maple against the blue sky? After all there has to be some gristle in a marriage to keep it from going stale. Nothing stale about Reed and Poppy! Happiness flowed back as Philip realized how precious their friendship was to him, and had been for twenty-five years now. These Sundays of hard play and good talk were anything but routine. Each remained an occasion, enriched by all the years of their companionship, yet as fresh and startling as the autumn itself. How splendid Mrs. Welch's chrysanthemums were this year!

He whistled a little tune as he walked along, swinging his racquet. Mr. Norton was out mowing his grass; Philip waved as he went by, and waved again at the Goldsteins on their bicycles. What a nice comfortable neighborhood it had become, though they all talked about moving "farther out"—talked about it, but had worked so hard over the years to make their gardens, put in swimming pools and tennis courts, had planted so many trees, that, really, there was no idea of doing so. Besides, where would they find this agreeable atmosphere? Nearly everyone gave a cocktail party for the neighbors once a year, but otherwise privacy was respected and when it came to the real things, they knew very little about one another. So what a shock when Reed's next-door neighbor, Ned Brokaw, was found to have juggled five million dollars from the bank of which he was president! This had happened in the past year and Philip, passing the house, wondered about it again . . . how did Ned imagine he could get away with it? It was as though a shark had suddenly surfaced in tranquil waters among the Sunday bathers. The trial was months away and Ned went about his business as though nothing had happened. The Brokaws even gave a big party one Sunday—the quiet street was suddenly lined with Cadillacs and Porsches, and the hi-fi blared till all hours.

"They are goons, that's all" was Poppy's verdict. "Caresse was simply never an authentic person."

"But was Ned your idea of an authentic cad?" Reed had teased.

And they were off on one of their battles, for Reed insisted that Ned had been caught juggling some money and was simply unlucky enough to be caught—hundreds of bank presidents probably did the same thing.

Philip quickened his pace, eager to find out what delicious concoction Poppy was cooking for their dinner, she the world's worst housekeeper but an excellent cook. He pushed open the door and called out, "Where is everybody?" No Mozart record was playing. The silence seemed strange.

"Reed?"

"I'm in here, Phil, in the library."

Reed was sitting at the big desk. He lifted his head and stared at Philip.

"What is it? Is Poppy sick?"

"Yes, in a way." Reed got up. His hands, holding two sheets of paper, were trembling. "I just got back from taking mother to church and found this on the desk. Perhaps you'd better read it yourself, while I change."

Philip took the two typewritten sheets and sat down on the green velvet sofa, Poppy's first extravagance when Reed began to make money years ago. It had faded, Philip noted. He was rattled. At first he could hardly concentrate on the words, but as he read on, he saw that this letter must be taken seriously.

Sept. 15th

Dear Reed,

I have not come to this letter and the decision it conveys easily or lightly. The seeds go back a long way in our marriage. Increasingly in the past years I have buried feelings of outrage and despair. And I must say now, before you read the rest of what I have to say, that I have decided a separation is necessary if I am ever to become a whole human being.

It seems quite useless to explain. I have tried many times to tell you what troubles me, only to be brushed aside, cajoled, or beaten down. You have, for a long time, appeared unable to look at yourself or to examine our relationship as it has deteriorated year by year. Was it ever really good after we fell out of love?

Lately sex has been a temporary and false means of allaying anxiety and of coming to a moment's rest. But I cannot believe that after twenty-seven years of marriage sex can be almost the only means of communicating—and if it is, there is no valid communication in it.

We have resented each other for a long time. We have not understood each other for a long time. There has been no meeting of minds even about politics for a long time. The Vietnam war separated us in some final and excruciating way. It is the best example I can think of of your need to avoid unpleasant truths, to cut yourself off from feeling anything that may prove disturbing. No doubt your success in business stems from this ability to cut off what might hurt or dismay *if faced.*

Our children have left home. I carried that responsibility to the end. And now I have come to understand that if I am ever to do serious work, it will have to be soon. I have about twenty years before me. You have never taken me seriously as an artist and that is, I know, partly my fault. I have found it difficult to believe in myself, let alone persuade you that "art is long, and time is fleeting." But I am determined now at last to get at it with all I have in me to give. It's a tremendous risk, but it is better than slow murder—or perhaps I should say "self-murder"—and that is what has been going on.

You will ask, Why now? What triggered this madness? My answer may mystify you, but it is the truth. The Watergate televised sessions, with all they revealed of how easily nice clean-cut young men could deceive themselves in a climate of power, was what shocked me into recognition. We cannot go on like this, I said to myself, and I meant you and me. Honesty has got to begin somewhere or we are going to be trapped in a public ethos so deadly that it has begun to poison even private lives. It is a long time since I have felt like an authentic human being. Perhaps you do. If so, that is one more reason why I have to go.

I have gone to mother's as a temporary measure. Later on I would like to study in England where there are sculptors I admire and could learn from, and later on to Italy to work with marble. I presume you will be willing to give me some support. I am not interested in marrying again. There is no one else. But a legal divorce may be best, for I do not intend to come back.

Poppy

Philip read the letter twice, then laid it on the desk and went to the French windows to stand looking out into the garden, to try to gather himself together. He felt slowed down as though he were swimming under water, unable to react quickly. Yet he must try to summon something to say when Reed came back. What help could he offer? He was in a state of violent inner disorder in which the only clear thing was that Poppy meant what she had written.

"So there it is!" Reed said, looking flushed. He had changed into shorts. "We'd better get out of the house. I can't stand it in here. Want a drink?"

"No thanks. A bit early, isn't it?"

"What time is it, anyway?"

"Half-past eleven."

They went out to the patio and sat stiffly in two armchairs. The marguerites Poppy had set out in five huge pots were still in profuse bloom, ragged mounds of pale yellow, and Philip commented on how well they had done.

"How can she wreck all this? Just walk out, for Christ's sake?" Reed pounded the arm of his chair with his fist.

Philip knew that anger was bound to be the first reaction, self-protective anger. "The letter makes it clear, Reed."

"What's clear about it? She doesn't know what she's doing. She hasn't the foggiest idea what it will be like to be on her own after all these years. Do you believe she's the great artist she imagines she is?" And, as Philip could not answer this, "Do you?" Reed insisted.

"I don't know."

"Exactly. Nobody knows, not even Poppy herself. She's used her so-called art as a weapon against me for *years*. Anything I wanted or needed that she didn't want she got out of by saying she had to work. And where did it get her? What did she accomplish, after all—even after we built her the studio? I wish I'd never done it."

"Come on, Reed, you did it because it was something Poppy wanted very much, and you love her."

"O.K. So I'm generous, and she walks out on me, walks out for no reason!"

"Well, she seems to have thought it out pretty carefully."

"It's a dirty trick."

"No." Philip was determined not to get into an argument, but he was not about to lie, either. And he wished Reed would stop shouting at him.

"Why didn't she say all this ages ago? Why bury it and spring it on me now? Apparently she's been lying to me for years. I've been going to bed for years with a woman who despised me. That's what it amounts to, can't you see? I've been had!"

"I don't think talking now is going to help, Reed. You're in a state of shock. I think I'd better go on home."

"Hell, don't go. I'll pull myself together," Reed muttered. Again he banged the arm of his chair with his fist, over and over, as though he were battering out words, ugly, angry words. And Philip, who had half risen, sat down again and waited miserably. It was like watching a big cat thrash around in a cage and being helpless to free the beast. Philip ran a finger round his collar, soaked through, he discovered. This is what is called "sweating it out," he thought.

"I suppose Poppy will have told the children?"

"How do I know? She didn't tell Emerson . . . I called him just before you came."

Yes, Emerson was the one he would tell, of course.

"He must have been pretty upset."

"His chief concern seemed to be whether I could send him a windbreaker he left in the hall closet. He did offer to come home, but what good would that do? He's trying out for the freshman soccer team. The children will be all right. Poppy chose her time well. I'm the one who gets hurt, you see. 'He who gets slapped'!" Reed laughed harshly.

And Philip sat there, perfectly still, waiting, the rock, he supposed, for the angry sea to batter itself against. And batter it did.

"This is what I get for having endured Poppy's rages, her migraine headaches, her depressions, for twenty-seven years! You know I've never had a wife in the ordinary sense of the word. Did Poppy entertain visiting firemen? Did Poppy have our friends in for cosy dinners? At the very suggestion of such a thing she took to her bed. Do you remember that time years ago, when we were to give a party for once, and she had to be hospitalized at the last minute? And left me with a huge sack of cabbages to be made into coleslaw? Good Christ, what a marriage!" Catching Philip's smile, for those cabbages were a *cause célèbre,* he shouted, "It's not funny, God damn it!"

"I know," Philip said gently. "I didn't mean it was. But those cabbages . . ." And suddenly they were both laughing a little hysterically. "We had cabbages coming out of our ears!" Because the tension had broken at last, he was able to say, "At least Poppy never bored you. Half the marriages I know are temples to boredom. You and Poppy stayed alive."

Reed was in no mood to admit that. He took another tack, man to man now, his tone confidential. "Why should I support her? I'd like to see Poppy earn her living for a change. What if I tell her, 'Fine. Go your own way. But you'll get no help from me'?"

"I don't know the law on that, but would you want to keep her as a prisoner?"

Reed flushed dark red. For a second he looked as though he were going to turn on Philip, but instead shook his head. "Let's play. We might as well."

Facing Reed on the court, Philip realized how much anger he had held back in the last half hour, and how fine it was to have a legitimate way to let the tension out. He felt fiercely alive down to his toes, as he delivered a hard, flat serve that Reed missed. They were nicely matched, but Philip often lost simply because he hadn't Reed's implacable will to win. Today he was determined to win. He enjoyed the steady, hard plop-plop of the balls, one after another. Even the sound of the game fitted his angry mood, and when Reed put over some high lobs he felt electric energy in his body as he ran back, putting out everything he had. Poppy had often called them a bear and a leopard, he remembered, and today the bear was heavy and the leopard full of fire. The leopard won the set.

Reed flung his racquet down. "God damn it, I can't even play tennis any more." He was panting.

"I thought you played well. We needed to let off steam, didn't we? Another set?"

"Not today. I'm done in. Let's have a beer."

Just as well, Philip thought. He himself was drained now, quite exhausted, as a matter of fact. He had a stitch in his side, and was glad to sit down on the terrace while Reed went in to get the beer. In this state of passive physical slump Philip had no defense against woe. Poppy's absence hung over him, and he realized that their Sundays together as a threesome would probably never happen again.

Reed handed him a bottle and a glass, and drank half of his own bottle in one gulp before he sat down. "I'm a bad loser," he said. "After all these years I don't have to tell you that."

"Winning's easier," Philip smiled. For a moment, as Reed sat down heavily, he thought that this man was not young. Reed was so highly charged and all of a piece that he had seemed young well into his forties. Now he looked his age, and in the suddenly perceived thickness of the jowls Philip saw something obtuse, something that age had not refined. Quite the contrary. What was there was force, at the expense of sensitivity. Yet Reed had intelligence, Philip reminded himself, that could grasp abstract ideas and put them quickly and ingeniously to work for him in his business. It was as though in the last hour Philip had had to look at this old friend in a new light. And he felt a kind of shame at making judgments. What had changed all of a sudden?

Reed interrupted these ruminations by turning toward him. "What does Poppy mean when she talks about Watergate as though it had something to do with me? With us? Isn't that just plain crazy? What connection can she make?" Reed's tone was speculative now, not angry.

"I can't explain it," Philip said, after a second's pause when he decided not to try. "But there is a clue there, I'm sure. Remember how furious she was when you defended Ned?"

"I was only teasing, Phil. You know that!"

"Poppy was serious. Maybe neither of us realized how serious she was."

"I get the sense that she just doesn't *like* me."

"Maybe you're lovable but not likable," Philip said quickly, to cover too hard a truth as best he could.

"What in hell do you mean by that?"

"Just thinking aloud."

"You've got to tell me."

"Do I?" Philip took a gulp of beer and, leaning back in the deck chair, half-closed his eyes. "Genius is tough on other people, and you're something of a genius in your way. But you're a good animal, and that's lovable."

"So?"

"Well, Reed, you're not really interested in what other people are feeling."

For once Reed did not react quickly. Then he said, "Feelings bore me. Is that a crime? Besides, for years I've come home from work not knowing what I would find—hysterical weeping, anger, no dinner, a burned dinner. I haven't complained."

"No, Poppy's done the complaining. I'll grant you that."

"I just can't see why she has to do this *now?* She's walking out just when the children have left. What am I to do in this huge place alone? Has she ever stopped to think of *me?*" Reed got out of his chair and paced up and down.

Philip didn't even try to answer. What was there to say? That Poppy had waited so long because she *did* think about Reed? To say that would only make things worse, humiliating.

"God damn it, Phil, it's been good in bed. Only last week . . ." But there Reed stopped, turned away, looked out into the garden. "What do you know about all that? You have no idea!"

"No one knows anything about a marriage, really, except the partners, does he? I mean, anyone outside is like a person walking outside a walled garden . . . he may hear a peacock scream or get a whiff of roses, but that's about all he can know."

"Roses?" Reed laughed his loud natural laugh. "Come on, let's eat. Poppy left a casserole ready. For once there's food. Let's eat!"

Philip felt Reed's hand on his shoulder, pushing him gently toward the house. Recognizing the warmth in that gesture, he was touched. Whatever happens, Reed and I are friends. But even as he took comfort in that thought, the realization of what it was going to mean—Reed and I *without Poppy*—took him by the throat. For the first time he faced the desolation for himself within this divorce. It was overwhelming, and as they walked into the silent, empty house, he suddenly felt sick. "Sorry," he murmured as he fled into the downstairs john, where he threw up his breakfast.

When he came out, Reed took one look at him and said, "Friend, you're shook up."

"Probably that virus that's going the rounds. I'm terribly sorry, old man, but I think I'd better get home."

"I'll drive you. But hadn't you better sit down a while first?"

"Thanks. I'll walk."

He was ashamed of the relief it was to get away. But you can't help people if you don't know where you are yourself, he thought. His head felt about five times its usual size and he walked slowly, tasting vomit in his mouth, feeling dizzy and weak. Walking head down, he almost passed his own gate. Then at last the bliss of being alone, of pulling the shades down and falling onto his bed. He took two aspirin, lay there, listening to the slow, labored thud-thud of his heart. If you are sick enough, you don't feel any pain. The irony of this thought made him smile, and after a while he dozed, and images of Poppy and Reed floated in, images from the past. It was as though he had not only been forced to throw up his breakfast, but also twenty-seven years of his life. Only the immediate present seemed quite unreal—his happy waking that morning, aeons ago, and his breakfast in the cool air with Perseus.

If only he could talk to Evelyn! But that was where Poppy had fled, so—not possible for the present. For the present they were all in limbo, a limbo for him of vivid images that refused to go away—the way Poppy listened to music, like someone drowning, so avid and so desperate was the starved person that music opened up. Philip saw her, her generous mouth slightly open, her hands clasped tightly on her knees, and remembered how many times at a concert he had felt he had to waken her, bring her back by touching her shoulder or whispering something in her ear, and how she had sometimes held his hand then, as though she were literally grasping a lifeline and would drown without it.

Philip groaned and turned over, only to have Reed pursue him—Reed when they had been working on the plans for the new building for the factory and had had such a marvelous time hashing things out, arguing, and finally working together at the drawing board, Reed's engineering skills and Philip's sense of functional beauty meshed. Had Poppy been a little jealous of them? She had gone upstairs while they had talked late into the night, fertilizing each other's imaginations like lovers. A great time, and it had ended in a very fine piece of architecture, the only thing Philip had built that had ever won a prize. How Reed had teased him about that and told him he had better take Reed into the firm as industrial consultant!

"Lovers?" The word came back. Well, in a way. He and Reed had for that time, a few months, been very close. They had talked for hours on the phone and the atmosphere had been electric because they were concentrated absolutely on one project. But whatever had happened, it had been all in the mind. And when it was over, it was over. Ten years ago now. Reed rarely even asked him what he was building these days. He was harassed by business worries, secretive, and on the defensive.

Philip tried to turn his mind off and rest by going back to happier times. Their trip to Greece—ten years ago—could it be? All three children had been in camp and Reed had rented a sailboat, so they could explore some islands on their own. Oh, those days of sailing, and the long lazy swims in perfect water, turquoise blue over very white sand, the smell of rock roses and little pine trees! It had been a week of heaven, except for one terrifying storm near Patmos. Suddenly the air had gone dark and a high wind had blown in from nowhere. The boat had broached and taken in a lot of water. Then Reed had shown his mettle, ordering Poppy and Philip to take in sail, while he put the ship into the wind, and somehow got them through the worst and into safe harbor.

"Reed, you were magnificent!" Poppy had said, and Philip never would forget the look she had given him. Had she ever looked at Reed with such admiration again? Not for years, anyway. It had taken "a jolly little storm," as Reed had called it. But in this sort of crisis, where what was required was expertise and guts, Reed was in his element. And Poppy could never imagine that he might have shown the same sort of command in his business affairs. No, she would never concede that. Especially not lately, when she had watched Reed coldly, like an enemy, analyzing, probing, expecting and believing the worst. And he himself had not been much help, he had to admit. No, nothing had been really the same since Vietnam.

Philip pushed two pillows behind his head and sat up. In that battle with his son, Reed had won, but at great cost to himself and to his marriage. He had used every weapon against Harry, as though being a C.O. was a family disgrace. And Harry had finally given in. That was a pity, and Philip often wondered why he had. Possibly to protect his mother? Possibly because he couldn't stand another wrangle between Poppy and Reed, and had chosen to go to war rather than suffer that awful tearing in the home? Harry was not a coward, but Philip had often thought that he was a yielder rather than a fighter, unlike his twin. In many ways Susie was the masculine one of the two, and one could see why Harry irritated his father, slouching around in jeans, his hair long, always lying down somewhere rather than sitting, his manner to his father patronizingly polite. Harry got under his father's skin, and it was mutual.

"My old man has the instincts of a prehistoric animal," he had said to Philip once. "He's not even human."

This was after he had come back, alive, and in a curious way unchanged, except that he now had the upper hand and used it—he came back with a store of scurrilous stories about the behavior of the army, about corruption everywhere, about millions of half-American Vietnamese children, homeless and battered. But as he told these stories he always smiled in a strange way, as if it didn't matter that much. His repeated question these days was "What did you expect?" Philip found him disturbing. Perhaps because in his own way he had cheated on himself, he had to look at everything with cynical amusement—was that it? Or was it that he just couldn't talk to people of Philip's generation? They were beyond the pale, it sometimes seemed. Yet Harry was working for Amnesty, and just once lately had lowered his guard about that in Philip's presence. How little we ever know about one another!

As all this flowed in and out, Philip wondered why people felt so strongly about family life—so much of it demanded the wearing of masks in order to keep the peace. Not Poppy, though. She had never worn a mask, he thought, not even when the twins were small, bumptious, charming, imaginative, begging for poems to be read aloud, making caves out of chairs and a blanket, hooting like owls, wrestling each other fiercely till one or the other howled for mercy. Philip remembered Poppy turning to him one day in the midst of some such scene of carnage, saying, "Try to have a conversation with these around!" She was convinced that no woman would have a child if she could foresee what the first six or eight years would be like. "It's not humanizing," she was fond of saying. "It's dehumanizing. One is simply a slave." Yet if he had not known her feelings, he would have thought her an exceptionally maternal woman. So perhaps, after all, she had worn a mask.

What if they'd had more money then? Money came when it was no longer needed. How often that happened! It had been the early years when Poppy needed a nursemaid, a cook, and all the rest. What had money done for her when it was there in abundance? Well, it had built her a studio. But. . . .

The room was half dark now. But Philip didn't turn on the light. His head still ached, and there was something suitable in this half-light, the loneliest hour of the day for those who live alone.

He lay there, sinking, sinking into loss, the loss of Poppy and Reed, almost as though he had been married to their marriage. He was deep inside their lives, and they, God knows, deep inside his. And at fifty one doesn't ever remake such a friendship, because its riches come partly from its long past—the small memories, the jokes, the old battles. How could Poppy throw it all away, tear it in two?

"Poppy," he murmured, closing his eyes against the pain behind them. Had he ever been in love with her, as he was sure Reed had suspected at one time? Yes, if being in love meant feeling with a person as though she were part of yourself. Yes, if feeling more alive with someone than with anyone else were it. But not if being in love meant a physical pull not to be denied. In a way he was too close to Poppy to be "in love." She disturbed him, but not in that way. What fascinated him was her quality of raw humanity, absolutely spontaneous. For her the simplest things became momentous because she lived her deepest self so close to the surface. This frightened and even outraged some people. It bored Reed. But for Philip it had—it was a curious comparison, he thought—the opulent, life-enhancing brilliance of certain early Matisse paintings. Not quite real—and yet more than real.

Poppy's reaction to any social situation was so extreme that she often appeared to be on some wild inner roller coaster. She overreacted in an absurd way, seeing insults where none were intended or bolting out a tirade with such dramatic force that a mere comment on a painter or even on the weather became a personal attack. Philip sat back and watched these scenes with the utmost delight, but Reed dreaded them. And it had to be admitted that they had a kind of zany violence for which Poppy herself paid with wakeful nights and shame. No wonder she shied away from giving dinner parties—the cost in psychic turbulence was immense.

Yet there was nothing he knew about this woman that led to the belief that a solitary life would be the answer, or that she was not now hurling herself into disaster through the illusion that she could make it as an artist. How little she knew of that competitive, cutthroat, fashion-controlled world of the galleries! And how did one break in at her age? "Oh, dear! Oh, dear!" Philip murmured, realizing as he heard his own voice what a very old-fashioned, spinsterish sound the phrase had.

Then it occurred to him that, after all, the chief motivation for her dramatic refusal to go on with Reed sprang as much from what she lumped together as "Watergate"—meaning, he supposed, general corruption and compromise with values she held essential—as from any conviction about herself as artist.

But was she right about Reed? Philip lay down again. Again he had the taste of nausea in his mouth. Who could afford to be as uncompromising as Poppy undoubtedly was? How much do we all overlook in one another to keep love—even friendship—alive? In middle age intransigence such as Poppy's was childish. Who is perfect? Who has not compromised somewhere along the line? They had often had this out.

"You could have been a really good architect," Poppy sometimes said. "Why did you settle for pleasing clients?"

"Why should I impose my ideas on a client? He's going to live in the house, after all."

But for Poppy it was simple. "It's like painting a work someone will want to see on his wall instead of what *you* see, isn't it?"

The phone beside the bed rang insistently. Full of dread, Philip made himself lift the receiver. It was bound to be Poppy. And it was.

"Pip? It's me. I suppose by now you know I've left Reed."

"I was over there this morning."

"Is he all right?"

"He's angry. What did you expect?" Philip knew his tone was cold. He simply did not know how to behave with Poppy.

"You sound cross."

"I'm in a state of shock, Poppy."

There was a second's silence before she said defiantly, "You can have no idea the relief it is for me."

"Maybe, but you've blown the roof off and it feels rather cold around here."

"We'll always be friends, Pip. Surely you know *that.*"

"I'll try to remember it."

"You're not going to take sides against me?" Philip could feel the anxiety flowing across the wires as a tangible thing. It was not, after all, going to be that easy for Poppy.

"I couldn't take sides against either of you. I'm stuck in the middle, and it's damned uncomfortable." Philip didn't want to be cross, but he found that he was, that it was quite impossible to be either gentle or warm. He agreed, because he could find no reason to refuse, to meet her for lunch the next day at a French restaurant near his office.

He did ask about the children before he hung up. The twins were absolutely on her side apparently, but Emerson had been upset. "He has always been a little pope like his father, you know," and Poppy's laugh was so clear and happy that it seemed to prove she really was free. "Let them think up decrees and encyclicals together."

But who would look after the house? Philip wondered, as he put the receiver down. He got up and went to the refrigerator for a glass of milk. How could Reed manage that big place alone? The days and months ahead were going to be filled with horrors of all kinds, especially mundane horrors about *things*, he foresaw. As he opened a can of cat salmon for Perseus—patient animal, it was long past his dinnertime—and set it down, he felt immensely weary as he faced what he would have to give.

Well, he told himself, taking the milk into the living room, this is what happens when you invest heavily in other people's lives. Why, then, did he have no wish at all to see Kathy, his own secret treasure and love of many years? Why not bury himself for a few hours in her warmth? He sat down heavily in a straight chair, and realized that he did not have that in him. He felt gutted.

Chapter II

Philip had been standing on the steps of Chez Pierre for ten minutes when Poppy finally turned the corner, her head bent against the wind, one hand holding her big red hat to keep it from blowing away, a black cape billowing round her.

"Hey, what wind!" she gasped, as she reached up to kiss his cheek. "It makes me feel like a whole wash hung up and thoroughly aired! Do you think this cape makes me look fat?"

"Not at all. Suits you."

"Good!" And she twirled around once to show it off. "I bought it this morning—that's why I'm late—to celebrate."

Philip censored his quick reaction to the word "celebrate" and said nothing until they were seated in a corner and had ordered drinks. Fussing about with the menu, he found himself inwardly in uncomfortable disarray. On the one hand, he was extremely glad to see Poppy looking so brilliant. On the other hand, he felt rage stirring below the surface, and rage, so unlike him, was frightening.

"To your freedom!" He lifted his glass, but did not meet her eyes.

"You're furious, of course." The words forced him to look at her and what he found in her eyes was tenderness and laughter.

"I don't know. I just can't get used to the idea, that's all. You'll have to give me time."

"All you are thinking about," she said lightly, "is the comforts you are going to miss. No man can stand domestic upheaval. It creates outrage. That's why women are so reluctant to go their own way."

"You know a great deal about it all suddenly." It was very irritating that Poppy had been able to put her finger so accurately on what he felt. How did she achieve this so fast, like a hummingbird darting in to a flower?

"I've always known it. I just buried it. Now that I'm free I can afford to admit what I've been aware of for years. Don't you see, Pip? Oh," she wailed, "if *you* can't see, who ever will?"

It had always charmed Philip that just when Poppy seemed most self-assured, she showed the crack in her armor, her vulnerability and self-doubt. But this time he could not reassure, praise, assent. He was far less objective than he had imagined himself to be. "I've been thrown off balance. I don't know what I feel."

For a moment there was silence. Poppy turned her glass in her strong hand, a sculptor's hand with a thick wrist. And Philip waited for the explosion or the laughter, or whatever mood she would dive into as a catalyst for emotion. She was good at this. But when she finally spoke, it was quietly, speculatively, as though the violence in her had come to rest.

"I've always thought of you as one thinks of Montaigne, someone wise and tender and safe from extreme emotion. And I have wondered how you achieved this—whether it was because of something missing, some human turbulence just not there to be reckoned with—"

"Thanks awfully!"

"Let me finish—or whether it was that you had transcended what most human beings have to suffer—rage, passion, unrequited love, the fever of unfinished work, whatever—and so had reached some higher range. I used to think you had, and how precious it was to contemplate, dear Pip, you'll never know."

"You put this angelic disposition of mine in the past."

"Well—" She lifted her head and looked him straight in the eye, then smiled and paused, distracted by laughter at the next table.

Philip lit a cigarette. He had dreaded tears or, worse, an armor of cynicism, but he had not been at all prepared to find himself examined or re-examined by a Poppy in such a controlled and luminous state. "Go on. Don't be distracted by that handsome man."

And again she turned toward him her penetrating look. "You see, Pip, now that the structure that held us all together—you, Reed, and me—is broken or laid aside, I begin to understand that we were what we were to one another out of weakness, not strength. You borrowed our marriage as some kind of 'home,' didn't you? And we borrowed your kind and loving presence to oil our wheels, to help make the rough passages a little smoother."

Philip had no answer for this. No doubt it was true. Or partially true.

"Reed needed a man friend like you far more than he needed a wife. Can't you see?"

"No, I can't," Philip said loudly, glad to be sure of something at last in this topsy-turvy conversation. "I don't see at all how he is going to get along without you." And again his anger dismayed him.

"He can hire someone to see that his clothes get to the cleaner's and his meals are cooked. He'll find out that he has to pay through the nose to get what he took for granted when I was his unpaid housekeeper, I can tell you!"

"Oh, dear!" Philip groaned.

"What's the matter?"

"We are in a forest of Women's Lib clichés and I simply cannot bear it—not from you, Poppy."

"Why not from me? Am I outside womanhood?" Then she broke into a wide smile, and the mood changed. " 'Womanhood' is such an odd word. Unhood a woman and what do you find?"

"A saint? A fury? An artist, perhaps?"

"Certainly not a saint!" Then she considered, and half closed her eyes. "I suppose you do think of me as a fury, smashing things to no good end, whereas I believe I have been a fury all these years because I didn't have the courage to admit defeat, and so took it out on Reed. I should never have married. I'm just not what a wife is supposed to be."

"And what is that? Isn't every fruitful marriage in some way unique? Are there rules?"

"Ours was not fruitful."

"Don't be ridiculous. You had three great children. Reed has been a kind of wizard in his business life, and you have worked in a beautiful studio I designed for you. What's unfruitful about all that?" His tone was sharp and Poppy reacted like a child to a governess.

"Nothing, I suppose." Then she looked up and shook her head like a willful horse. "Except that I felt drained all the time."

"Drained of what, exactly?"

"Drained of myself, Pip—of my true self. I was always pretending, always acting, trying to soothe, placate, support, be what a wife is supposed to be."

"Maybe Reed felt he was placating and soothing also. Maybe marriage always has a little of that in it. Marriage has always seemed to me one of those impossibles that men work at in the wild hope that this one, theirs, is going to prove that the impossible can be achieved."

"O.K., except that it's usually women who work at it." And Poppy laughed her free loud laugh that always made heads turn in her direction. "I just remembered one of my father's favorite phrases, 'the faith of our fathers and the *work* of our mothers.' Little did he know!"

"Did you mind when they divorced?"

"No, not at all. At last I could see them separately, without all the tensions, and really enjoy them. You can't imagine how awful the atmosphere at meals was when I was growing up—Mother in her icy brilliance trying to get a rise out of Dad, and his deliberate brutal indifference. You see, I was really tortured by the marriage. I wanted to love my father, but he behaved so badly. He even resented mother's job and the money she made to put me through college!"

"He was rather unworldly, I suppose."

"Unworldly?" Poppy opened her eyes wide. "He was just like Reed about money—generous when something was his own idea, furious about what daily living cost, and unwilling ever to discuss it. My father's face became red at the word 'money.' It was *the* emotional subject in our family, and it wrecked that marriage—and, I suppose, made me the careless spendthrift that I am." There was a pause while the waiter deboned their sole and served them. "I feel so old sometimes," Poppy said, attacking her sole as though she had not eaten for days.

Philip was always amused and delighted at the way Poppy ate, drank, and talked, with such enormous appetite and zest.

"Why are you smiling?" she asked, catching his amused, indulgent look. "You are almost human for the first time since we walked in here."

"You have the greatest capacity for enjoyment of anyone I ever knew. You're more alive than anyone else, Poppy—even to the way you devour a sole."

"Thanks. Most of the time I feel starved, I must admit."

Philip recognized at this moment that if he were asked to define Poppy in one word, it would have to be "hunger"—hunger for life, hunger for flowers, food, hunger for expression, hunger, no doubt, for love. Or was it for something else, something she called her "art"? It was not possible to be angry with Poppy for long, and Philip felt the anger in him flowing away as he watched her eat.

"You may feel old," he said, "but you look very well—about ten years younger than your statistical age."

"Do you think Reed will give me a generous settlement?" she asked out of the blue.

"I have no idea. At present I think he wants to punish you. He is warding off pain with anger these days."

"Mother says to count on nothing. She wants me to get a job and prove I can manage on my own. But I have so little time, Pip!" she said, catching his look before he himself realized that he agreed with Evelyn. "I can live on very little."

"Even though you're a careless spendthrift?"

"Don't tease. If I have to, I can. Especially in England."

"England is damned expensive from what I hear."

"Why should I accept a mean settlement? I've been a worker in Reed's house for twenty-seven years at no salary!"

"Reed is hardly in the mood to go along with that."

"I'll get a lawyer who can stand up to him."

For a few moments Philip's gloom had lifted under Poppy's spell, but now the sense of waste and loss came back, and with it his anger. "You'll never have a home again. I suppose you realize that."

"What do you mean by a 'home'? I've been living way beyond my means as an artist for years, Pip. I've wasted time taking care of the place, gardening, vacuuming, cleaning the pool. I wouldn't mind living in one room for the rest of my life, if it was possible to work in peace."

"You'll miss the garden."

"I had a garden, but I didn't have myself," Poppy shot back, and Philip saw she had flushed. "Of course I'll miss it."

"The daisies in those big pots did awfully well this year."

"Don't do that!"

"Do what?"

"Don't make me look back."

"Better look before you leap, Poppy." A new thought rose as Philip sensed his advantage. "Have you ever thought of a compromise?"

"What kind of compromise?"

"A Persephone kind. Go to England for six months and come home for six months." Philip didn't dare raise his eyes. He felt it to be an inspired plan, but if he moved now Poppy would dart away like a deer, surprised.

After a considerable pause Poppy said, "No. Compromise in the past is what is driving me to go away altogether, can't you see? It would never work. I'd just be split in two all over again in a different way. You must understand that, Pip, can't you?"

"I can't honestly see what you have to gain by cutting yourself off from a life you have worked at for twenty-seven years. Do you really believe you are going to succeed as a sculptor?" It was a sharp thrust and Philip winced at having resorted to it. But he felt irritated, irritated with this woman whom he watched put three envelopes of sugar into her coffee with majestic indifference to her weight. And, as though she felt his unfriendly eyes upon her, she lifted her head and looked quite severe.

"What is 'success,' anyway? I'm not even thinking

in those terms. The art world, from what I can make out, is as corrupt, perhaps more so, than the world of politics. But even if it were not, of course I don't think I'm a genius about to burst fully armed on a waiting army of critics and museum directors. I'm not a fool."

"Well, if you are not going to make a professional life, what are you going to do?"

"I want to find out what I have in me to be—and I guess for me 'being' is working at a piece of sculpture. If someone likes it after it is done, so much the better. But do you really think any artist works *first* for recognition, Pip, honestly?"

"In my impure art I don't even begin to function until someone wants a building. So I guess I don't know."

"Now you're cross again."

"Yes, I am cross. I really can't understand, since you have a studio and all day to work in it alone, why that isn't enough? Why do you have to uproot, leave Reed, tear his world to pieces to be yourself?"

"Why does it make you so angry? It's not your life."

"It *is* my life—that's what I've found out ever since Reed handed me your letter. A divorce is an earthquake, Poppy. It affects everyone anywhere near. I've never been shaken by anything in my life as I am by this."

"So Reed gave you my letter. Well, that's no surprise."

"We three have been members of one another for a long time, Poppy. And he was in a state of shock."

"He will never understand what I tried to say, but

perhaps you can. I mean about the Watergate mess having driven me, finally, to be honest with myself."

"Can you explain a little more? I'm not sure I do understand. Watergate is a political matter and you appear to be translating it and its effect into such private and personal terms." Philip knew that he sounded pompous, but Poppy's total disregard of his confession that he too had been hurt by the divorce had brought on an attack of reserve. She seemed very far away.

And, as though she really were far away, she lit a cigarette and looked around her for a moment. Then she sighed.

"When Reed and I were married, he was a struggling engineer and I was a struggling artist, and we could talk about things. But as I got absorbed in the children and he got really involved and started his own business, it seemed as though he were way out somewhere ahead of me, hardly looking back, and not caring at all what was becoming of the artist in me. And as he charged on, more and more successful, I fell back. But that wasn't the worst of it, Pip. The wives of most successful men are better off in blinders, and I don't wear them. I think our marriage began to wither about fifteen years ago when Reed fired half his men to recoup his losses. From a business point of view that was a highly successful operation, I gather, since he put in the swimming pool the next year. But by then I had begun to feel like the men he had fired—that my values and I were irrelevant."

"Yes," Philip said quietly, "I see. I really do." She

had become, he thought, extremely logical and, he had to admit, persuasive. "Did you ever try to tell Reed what you felt about that episode at the factory?"

"I didn't even tell you, Pip, as you know. I buried it and pretended it had never happened."

"But that wasn't quite fair. I mean, Reed might have explained that firing half the staff might be cruel, but firing the whole staff and going into bankruptcy wouldn't have helped anyone, would it?"

"It did something to Reed. He had to close off part of himself to do it, and it was that part, maybe, that included me. Oh, I don't know . . ."

Philip was relieved to be talking at last about something definite, rational, something that could be argued on a level where the subconscious beasts and angels did not threaten to erupt and take over. Catching her pleading glance, he reached over and took her hand. "Poppy darling."

But she withdrew it. "I'm not darling, not darling at all. Maybe I'm wrong about the factory, but you have to admit that Reed was obtuse and tyrannical about Harry and the war."

"Yes, he was. You know I did my best to keep him from exerting that kind of pressure."

"It was a public relations matter—you know that as well as I do. He couldn't take the flak of having a C.O. son and he made that an issue. It was beastly and dirty." Her words struck Philip like harsh sleet. There was to be no relief after all. "You're looking at your watch. I suppose you have to go."

"In a few minutes."

"The point is that Reed represents things I hate—and I'm afraid they are things I associate with masculine power."

"Whatever that is."

Poppy laughed, brought back to the present moment from her bitter journeys into the past, Philip thought, as she looked at him quite tenderly for a change. "It is not something you exhibit, dear heart. Thank God for that."

"No, I expect I exhibit an infernal ability to compromise about everything. Not very pretty, is it?"

"You're human, the most human being I've ever known. That's rare, Pip, very rare. You know, even my mother is not quite human sometimes. She's too omniscient. But you always are. You're open and gentle. How did you become you?"

"By being a bit cynical about absolutes. By seeing almost every truth as relative."

"You're evading me because I've embarrassed you. But it's all right, so long as you don't abandon me."

Philip was doing a sum in his head to decide about the tip and he nodded a little vaguely.

"You won't, will you?"

"Won't what?"

"Abandon me?"

"Of course not. Don't be a silly fool."

They walked to the corner arm in arm. Then Philip broke away—he was fifteen minutes late for an appointment. He walked fast, not looking back, but he was finding it difficult to extricate himself from the image of Poppy, so alive and well, leaving ruin around her.

How can she be so blithe about it all? Above all, so

sure of herself? And he had to admit that he missed the troubled, impetuous, willful Poppy who had so often cried on his shoulder. For he felt he was being dragged out to sea by an undertow over which he had no control—submerged and drowned, or nearly, by the force of his emotion. And Poppy had paid no attention to his cry of despair. It was as though she refused to listen, didn't want to know what he was going through over this separation. I simply must see her mother, he thought. I have to talk to Evelyn.

Chapter III

Philip walked up and down the house, waiting for Evelyn to arrive for a drink—she was never on time. The air had turned chill. It would not be comfortable on the terrace, and he lit the fire and talked to Perseus, who was already acting like an indoor winter cat, curled up in the brown velvet armchair.

"Bad things should not take place in the autumn, Perseus. It's all cracking up around us—we're getting old. I hate the falling leaves. I hate the rain. I hate everything."

Since the luncheon with Poppy, Philip had seen Reed twice, had talked on the phone with Harry and Susie, the twins, and had written to Emerson. He often felt like someone who has been given an impossible jigsaw puzzle to put together. Nightmare and confusion attended his sleeping and waking, and he had several dreams about being locked in and unable to get out, or of trying to pack for a journey and being unable to find his clothes. He woke from these dreams in a sweat. He found it difficult to concentrate on his work, had even been unaccountably brusque with a prospective client. The ludicrous truth appeared to be that he was far more upset by the divorce than either of the protagonists or their children. Yet his role was clearly to listen to one, then the other, to listen and sympathize—and not, if possible, take sides. If the divorce was settled in court (as everyone hoped it would not have to be), he would inevitably be a witness. Then would he have to take sides?

At last he heard Evelyn's car door slam and there she was at the door, cool and crisp. He was so glad to see her he lifted her right off her feet, kissed her, and set her down again.

Evelyn laughed. "If you're six feet tall, of course you can do that and get away with it!"

"It's just that I am desperately glad to see you. But you're light as a feather. You'll blow away one of these days."

It was one of Evelyn's charms that she made men feel delighted with themselves, Philip thought, as he left her to make vodka martinis. What an elegant creature she was! Not a beauty, not at all, but she had remarkable gray eyes and a look of the twenties in her casque of silver hair and in her style, and Philip enjoyed looking at her, as though she were a work of art, as she undoubtedly was.

How could she be Poppy's mother? They were absolutely unlike, even as physical types. Evelyn must have seemed complete even when she was a girl, and Poppy would always be "on the way," never "finished." Poppy was large and warm, Evelyn slim and cool, and if she had a maternal side it showed solely in the amused respect with which she had treated her only child. No sculptor would have drawn her portrait holding a baby . . . well, Philip said to himself, that's an odd thought!

When he came back with the drinks, Philip caught Evelyn for a second unaware, absorbed in a book about Le Corbusier, and in that second was shocked to realize that she had grown old . . . she who had seemed ageless well into her sixties. Yet when she lifted her head and smiled, the wrinkles, the angularity of her thin body were suddenly irrelevant as Evelyn, the person, looked at him now with her meditative look, and seized on his mood with unerring perspicacity.

"You are bearing the brunt, Philip, aren't you?"

"Yes, I suppose I am."

"The trouble with divorce is that it brings out the infantile, as I well know."

"In Poppy?"

"Poppy's like a small child running away from school." Catching her smile, Philip laughed for the first time in days. They laughed together, without meanness.

"And Reed?"

"Reed is behaving like a small boy whose marbles have been stolen and who wants them back."

Philip chuckled at the *double-entendre* she had certainly not intended, but she caught it then, of course. "Oh, well, you know what I mean. But maybe he does feel castrated. Who knows? Reed is very naïve in some ways, and quite defenseless."

"Has he talked with you? He wanted to."

"I think that had better wait, Phil."

"He says you are his best woman friend."

"I guess he'll have to make do with his best man friend for the present."

"It doesn't seem quite fair."

"What? That you should be left holding the bag, or that Reed is deprived of my dubious capacity to advise him?" But now she was suddenly serious. "As far as the divorce goes, I might as well tell you that I am on Poppy's side."

Philip was startled into anger in spite of himself. "How can you be? It's such a waste!"

Evelyn gave him a quizzical look. "Sit down and calm down, Phil. It's not your marriage, after all."

"Sorry. I'm on edge." Philip lifted Perseus out of the chair to an enraged miaow, and tried to persuade the big cat to settle down again on his lap. But Perseus walked away stiffly and disappeared into the kitchen. "The whole thing has made me quite ill."

"I expect it has. It's rather hard to be a universal wailing wall." Looking into the fire, Evelyn sipped her drink. Then she said quite severely, "But you can't afford to get involved so deeply—it's *not your life*."

"That's just it. It *is* my life, Evelyn, in a way."

"You mean that you were a member of the wedding and have remained so?" She lifted an eyebrow, and Philip had to admit that he had taken a great deal for granted that was strange, to say the least. She had him on the defensive.

"We had marvelous rapport, all three of us. We had so much fun together, Evelyn! Anything wrong with that?"

Evelyn did not answer quickly. She sipped her

drink. The fire held them for a moment in its bright presence. And when she spoke, it was with deliberate gentleness, though the words were harsh. "Perhaps you will agree that a marriage that survives at least in part because of the presence of a third member is a crippled marriage."

"But if it worked? And for twenty-seven years it seemed to."

"Yes, I suppose it did—at very great cost to you, Phil. You took up the slack. You understood. Poppy could confide in you and not feel disloyal because she knew you loved Reed. Reed trusted you and seems to have been able to accept your intimacy with his wife. But you never married."

"I'm not the marrying kind, for God's sake!" It was really a bit much if he was now going to be accused of not marrying as though it were a crime. "If I had wanted to marry I would have done so. I've led a happy and rather untroubled life till now, if you must know."

"I would say that you had invested too much in their lives, too much, perhaps, for the sake of your own growth. I'm not judging, Philip. I hope you know that I'm very fond of you."

Evelyn did not often utter her feelings, and the fact that she did at this moment broke Philip's reserve completely. He put his head in his hands and groaned. "I'm in hell, Evelyn. I feel I've been in an earthquake, still am. I feel undone. Half the time I can't even concentrate on a barnlike studio I am trying to design for a client." When he lifted his head, he laughed harshly. "Meanwhile, Poppy celebrates her freedom!"

"She has a long road to go before she has proved it

to herself. Let her enjoy a brief moment of relief before the real test comes." It was said quite sharply. Then Evelyn turned back to him with her relentless gentle demands on his reason. "Seriously, Phil, you have got to accept this event and go on from there, for your own sake—and for Poppy's too. She has made up her mind and she's not going to change it."

"I know that," Philip said miserably.

"I suppose you have considered moving in with Reed."

"It wouldn't work. He needs a wife, not a male nurse."

"Exactly. And you need a mature friend, not a sick child. Reed has a lot to learn about himself. Maybe in time you'll all three do some growing—and what else is life all about anyway?"

"Thanks. I have no wish to grow," Philip said, laughing at himself now. "I thought I was all grown up till you came and scolded me."

"How is Reed taking it?" Evelyn asked, as the mood changed to one of greater ease between them.

"Angry. Put upon. Incapable of seeing that Poppy has a case. He just does not understand—he never has." Philip stretched out his legs and, with his hands behind his head, stared at the ceiling. "It's not his fault exactly. After all, Poppy married him, and he hasn't changed. He's the same person she married, only more so. Why did she marry him, anyway?"

"She was twenty-three, an art student terrified of her gift, terrified that she didn't have the real thing. And Reed is a very attractive man, though not perhaps," Evelyn hesitated for the fraction of a second, "a good lover."

Philip shot up out of his chair and disappeared into

the kitchen to get the shaker and pour Evelyn and himself a second drink.

"I shock you, don't I?"

"Of course you do. I'm as nervous as a witch when it comes to talk of sex." Philip smiled, "Just another sign, I suppose, of retarded growth."

"All I meant was that Reed has a blunt sensitivity. He's unaware of his effect on other people because he has no antennae out, and, at the risk of startling you again, I think a person who can't know what other people are feeling is bound to be a bad lover. Reed strikes me as the kind of man who really believes that a woman wants to be mastered."

"Some women do."

"No doubt," Evelyn said drily. "But not, I think, my willful natural phenomenon of a daughter."

And they laughed. "The relief it is to talk with you, Evelyn!"

"At age seventy-six one ought to be able to provide some relief to a very young man."

"But seriously, Evelyn, I've sometimes imagined that Poppy did want to be mastered—that she was asking for it, like a child with tantrums."

"Poppy has a long way to go before she finds out what she really wants."

"But, Evelyn, she's fifty! You sound as though she had infinite time."

"Growth, curiously enough, sometimes happens very fast, given the right environment, loam, or whatever. Think of the way boys sometimes shoot up a foot in a year. That's a physical process, but things happen in the psyche in the same way exactly. I doubt if Poppy marries again . . . but if she does, she might learn that there is a difference between brute power and mastery. Who knows? And if she goes her own way alone, as I think she means to, well, there's always Grandma Moses to remember."

Out of the laughter Philip suddenly felt able to ask the crucial question. "Do you believe in Poppy's talent?"

It was not a question that Evelyn would answer lightly or evade, and Philip waited quietly while Evelyn sat up, brushed her hair aside with a familiar gesture, then leaned her chin on her hand. "In the first place, she's wasted thirty years being an amateur in an art that demands slow constant work if anything at all is to be achieved. I mean, it's not like a water color that can be dashed off when the spirit moves, don't you agree? There's a glimmer, there's a possibility, but who can say at this point? I don't believe Poppy herself has any illusions, but her sense of herself is bound up in sculpture and always has been. So whether she succeeds in the worldly sense doesn't really matter. What matters is that she feel fulfilled as a human being."

"I'm sick to death of all this talk of fulfillment at the expense of everyone else." He sounded peevish, even to himself.

Evelyn smiled indulgently. "It does get tiresome, but then so did Poppy's moods, despairs, illnesses—"

"I'm also sick and tired of bad art perpetrated in the name of self-expression, fulfillment, or whatever." Philip caught himself, seeing how difficult he was being. "I'm sorry, Evelyn. I'm battering at you, but it's because I need to understand."

"Yes, I know. Well, let me say then that one odd

thing about Poppy is that she does not mess around when she is working in the studio. There she is disciplined, careful, slow, and very severe with herself. And perhaps that is what makes me want to believe that she can and will achieve something, given twenty years or so."

"Oh, dear, she is so lovable," Philip said, scratching his head.

"Do you really think so? I wonder why." Evelyn smiled her mischievous smile. She was leading him on and he enjoyed it.

"Because she's innocent. She is really and truly innocent." He was thinking so hard that he realized suddenly he had been silent for some seconds. "Sorry. I was thinking."

"Go on. Tell me."

"There's no reserve, no barrier, between Poppy and whatever she is experiencing at the moment. So when you are with her, everything becomes fresh, unexpected, and delightful. Nothing in her response is jaded. Of course, that means that she often overreacts. I just don't know any middle-aged people like her. She's honest—and who else is, Evelyn?"

"Does Reed see that? Does he want it around?"

"I'd say yes to the first question and to the second I'm afraid I'd have to say no—at least in relation to himself."

Evelyn nodded and was silent.

"You see, for Reed marriage is a fortress. He wants to feel safe inside it with his wife and friends. He thinks, I suppose, that he has enough battles to fight outside in the world where he operates. So he is outraged if he is attacked at home. I can imagine feeling that way myself."

"Yes, but we are talking about growth and I'm afraid Reed stopped growing some years ago. Perhaps it happened over Harry. What do you think?"

"That was a disaster."

"At that point he walled himself in."

"Yes, he did." The illness of that time flowed back like poison into Philip's head. "The war did something awful to almost everyone. It bore in like a dentist's drill. And almost everyone turned away from the pain. In one way or another, Evelyn, half the people I know, myself included, never allowed themselves to imagine what we were doing. We couldn't let it in and live with it."

"Maybe. But not everyone sent a son into that war who wanted to be a C.O. Reed forced Harry's hand—and maybe Harry was weak to let that happen. But I can't condone it, Phil. It was a bad business." She got up, a little stiffly, and Philip rose to give her a hand. "I'm sorry, Phil." She lifted her face to be kissed. "But I don't think I can help Reed."

"Don't go yet!" It would be too lonely after she left. "And please don't shut Reed out. He needs you badly."

"Oh, I don't know."

"Reed says you're the only woman who ever really understood him. You can't abandon him, Evelyn. It would be cruel." Philip realized that his intense need to try to mend the wounds was because he himself could not bear the disruption, and he stopped short. "You're right—it's not my life and it's time I shut up about it."

"Don't worry. I expect the ice will melt in time." Then she added lightly, "For some unknown reason I'm fond of Reed in spite of everything."

"Thanks."

"Dear me, I feel quite tottery after those martinis."

"Stay for dinner. I'll make you an omelet."

"No, thanks just the same. I promised Poppy I'd be home for dinner, and she is cooking and brewing at this moment."

"Drive carefully."

"I will. Good-by, dear Phil. You are quite a comfort."

Philip stood in the door and watched the taillights waver a little at the gates, then swing out and disappear. The wind was chill and he was glad to go back into the house and to the fire and to Perseus, who had climbed back into the velvet chair. For a long moment Philip sat where Evelyn had sat, listening to the silence of the house, that acute silence after voices have come and gone, that silence in which the words just said reverberate and sometimes hurt. Was Evelyn right that he should have married, that he had let himself be seduced into a minor role around Reed and Poppy, and for the wrong reason—out of laziness or the fear of responsibility? Or because he had remained an adolescent all these years? He would have liked to ask Reed over for supper, but not the Reed who would rage and curse his wife—no, the old Reed, eager for a game of tennis and some good impersonal talk about politics or business. Was there never to be such a haven again? What was he going to do with his life now? Just work and come home alone and look at the news?

Too restless and frustrated to think about cooking a meal, Philip went out for a walk. The dank autumn smell fitted his mood, and somehow it was not so lonely out of doors. Was it, he wondered, because nature is on such a large cycle and so impersonal that, alone with trees and grass and a few late flowers, as he was in the dusk now, we are literally taken out of ourselves? Whatever the reason, he did find comfort in the sharp cry of a jay.

Chapter IV

Philip relaxed in his seat on the plane to Minneapolis. What relief it was to get out of the actual area where he had suffered so much pain and dismay for the last two weeks! Relief too, to be on his way toward an interesting job—to discuss plans for a new Unitarian church with his friend Chris Lawrence, the minister, whom he had known even before college when they were at St. Mark's together. Maybe he could put the whole sad divorce out of his mind for forty-eight hours. Familiar landmarks were fading out below him and, already about a hundred miles from Boston, he understood the value of distance, concrete distance, and what it did to help him find his balance. There should be some way, he felt, to achieve this detachment in the mind, but he had not found it lately. Could one ever look down on human affairs as one looks down on a landscape from a plane, forget small details, anxieties, angers, and see clearly only the great nourishing rivers, the large contour of hill and valley?

When the earth had become simply a dim brown expanse far below, he lay back and closed his eyes—and at once he was before a kind of mental television screen that brought him sequences of images, as though he were dreaming, for they came, seemingly irrelevant, out of his childhood.

He saw his mother sitting on the dunes back of the beach at Ogunquit in the shade of a big umbrella. She was embroidering something, her face in shadow under a white Panama hat, her hands swift and yet patient at the same time. He watched them from where he lay on his stomach in the sand, and wished she would pay more attention to him. For they were having a heart-to-heart talk, and he was a little jealous of that embroidery.

"You're hard on Dad," she was saying. "He's a stag at bay these days, Phil. We have been nearly ruined. You must try to understand him. You're nearly ten years old, after all."

But Phil was off and away on a fantasy, trying to slip the image of a stag against his red-faced, cross father, getting off the train in a Palm Beach suit and asking impatiently, "Where is Beth, boy? Where's my wife?"

"Phil, are you listening? Please pay attention!"

"He's not a stag. He's a bear, and he told me himself bears are bad-tempered and dangerous."

She had laughed then, and laid down the embroidery at last. "Of course he's a bear, but a very loving one."

"It's not loving to cut my pocket money."

"Darling, we are having to cut down everywhere. I'm doing the cooking myself, and on very little money these days."

"But I can't save enough for that bike now. It just isn't possible!"

It was nothing—a little scene on the beach that must have been repeated in one form or another on dozens of beaches that year of the depression. Why did it come back now, poignant, like a piece of music that brings with it reverberations from the personal past? Yet he could never think of his mother without anguish, and why was this? Because, dead now, she was forever unattainable, and while she lived she had filled his heart? A state of affairs, he had to admit, that would have given an analyst a field day. The fact was that his mother had a kind of brilliance that Philip would not find again—a brilliance of response, of being wholly present at any moment to whatever need was before her, of getting inside another person and letting them know it with the lightest possible touch, not probing and also never astonished. He had been drawn to Poppy, he often thought, because she had something of this, but she was too anguished herself to be capable of the merry detachment that had been the wisdom of his mother. Poppy could not be wholly relied on.

Also, Poppy was not a wit and his mother was. Like many shy people his mother hid her shyness under laughter, and especially under a talent for mimicry. His mother too was very much of a social character who thrived on good conversation and whose dinner parties were famous. How often he had lain in his bed on those evenings, listening with a pain in his stomach to the marvelous grown-up laughter downstairs!

Philip sat up and lit a cigarette. Would he have married if he had ever met a girl like Beth? And do men really try to marry their mothers? Reed certainly had done exactly the opposite. Evelyn had accused him of not marrying because he had never grown up. It seemed rather old-fashioned of her and had taken him by surprise.

But Evelyn could not keep him now from basking for a half hour in memories that soothed and delighted—memories of his mother and of his Aunt Agatha, her sister, a painter, a tiny dynamo of a woman who used to take him to the zoo, and to grown-up plays, and to the opera (she even gave him a top hat and an opera cloak when he was fourteen), and for great feeds at expensive restaurants—for Aunt Agatha was a very successful woman, and by the time of the depression had stowed away enough not to be affected by it. And, after all, she had never married and no one accused her of not being grown-up! If they had, she would have given them one of her sharp cool glances and chuckled as if to make clear that she felt very well off as she was and had no intention of changing. She was really serious only about her work, only deeply involved there, and there she closed the door. She refused to talk about it. Almost the only time Philip saw her angry was once when he had casually looked at some canvases that were stacked facing the wall.

"Don't you dare do that again, Philip! Those things are not to be seen—not by anyone."

"Why not? They looked interesting," Philip had summoned courage to answer.

"They're my failures. I keep my failures to myself—and learn from them. But you are never to do that again. Is that clear?"

It was clear, and it had increased his respect for Aunt Agatha.

No wonder his standard of feminine charm was high. He had been bathed in a very special radiance as a child—that of two women of exceptional quality. Where ever again would he find the ripple of their laughter, their spontaneous, irresistible mockery of pretension of any kind, their subtle, complex discriminations about value? Beside them he could place only Evelyn, but he did not believe for a moment that Poppy was right when she accused him of wishing to be a perpetual *cavalier servante* to some older woman whom he adored. Age had nothing to do with it, he thought; quality was the point. In his mother it was unself-conscious, humble even, and that was what made it irresistible. She never for a moment believed in her own superiority, though she would have defended to the death Agatha's right to feel superior.

His mother had not been a snob in the social sense. She and Agatha would have understood what it was about Kathy that had moved him so powerfully. They would have teased him a little, no doubt, but they would have understood. At least, he imagined they would. They would have seen that Kathy, middle-aged, a police detective (of all things!), divorced, childless, had touched him in a way none of his girls had ever done when he was a young man. Once he had told Reed about her, and Reed too had seemed to understand, and also to accept that he wanted to keep

Kathy a secret, even from Poppy—perhaps most of all from Poppy, who might have probed too deeply, who might have resented her, who knows? Yes, Reed had understood in a man-to-man way, but not the essence, which was mysterious even to Philip after ten years. Had anyone ever before loved as they did? Had anyone ever before read Dickens aloud after making love? Had any lovers laughed as much? Or cooked such delightful meals? Had such *fun?*

Philip opened his eyes. It was painful to wake from all these dreams and realize that he could not bring himself to see Kathy now. He felt impotent.

On an impulse he had called her from the airport before he left, to tell her briefly about Reed and Poppy and that he was too upset and cross for human company.

"Well, when you're not cross, come back. I've missed you" was her response. What a satisfactory woman! She never put pressure on him and that was partly because she was extremely busy at her job. She never asked to meet his friends or to enter his world. She had no sense of inferiority, but she was a realist. "It wouldn't work," she said, "Everyone would try too hard, myself included. Let's stay as we are, Phil."

She was admirable. He felt sure his mother and Aunt Agatha would have relished her forthrightness, and would have loved her as he did for her embattled defense of women—"those kids," as she often said, "whose brothers pimp for them before they're fourteen—pathetic, usually with low I.Q.'s, lazy often, corrupted, you see, and defenseless." Kathy was furious at the lack of decent correctional institutions. "They get out and are back on the street twenty-four hours later."

Philip had always supposed that one reason Kathy never bored him—and he hoped he never bored her—was just that whenever they met they exchanged two such totally different lives. They traveled happily in each other's lands, as it were, and that sense of travel, of escape from one's own routine, was partly what made the whole relationship alive and memorable like a holiday. Every one of their meetings in the last ten years had had a great sweetness and excitement for him, more than he could ever tell her or explain to himself.

Partly, it was freeing. But freedom from what? That was the puzzling question. And why had he felt it impossible to see Kathy since the separation? What was really happening to him?

For one thing he was possessed by anger. He had never been angry for more than a short half hour, and even that rarely. Now the anger was always there, and rose up over nothing at all—an incompetent waiter, an undecided client. He had lost control of his anger. Why in hell, if Poppy was going to do this, had she waited for so long? There was something revolting in springing such an act on a middle-aged husband. After all, what could Reed do with his life at this point? Marry again? Reed, Philip knew, was far too preoccupied with the factory to have time and emotional space for getting to know someone else. Women had never interested Reed very much. He had no women friends except Evelyn. God knows he might rush out and pick up some little chit in a moment of desperation—and that thought made Philip shudder. Bad as things were now, it would be impossible to see Reed at all if he married again. But how long could a man sustain himself on work alone? Especially since the children were not much comfort—Reed had alienated the twins forever over Vietnam, and Emerson, after all, would not be at home except on holidays, and even then could be expected to take off for Europe with a knapsack in the summer.

But Philip had to admit finally that his anger was ninety percent rage that his own stable, comfortable life, so carefully compartmentalized, had been thrown into grief and disorder. So, he told himself grimly, you are male chauvinist pig, after all. Yes, clearly, his anger, the irrational frightening anger (as opposed to his reasonable anger with Reed for being mean about a settlement), was directed against Poppy.

She wanted her freedom, freedom to become her real self, she had said in the restaurant eating Dover sole like a starving person. But who is free in this world? Everyone by the time he is fifty is hemmed about with restrictions and responsibilities. Freedom in Poppy's head was a theoretical state like an old-fashioned "heaven" that had, as far as Philip could see, no reality—a romantic illusion. She was engaged in a love affair with herself and the image that crossed Philip's eyes was that of a snake biting its own tail.

Sweat started out on his forehead. He lit a cigarette, only to see the No-Smoking sign flash on and hear the pilot's voice announcing the start of the descent to the Twin Cities. So he put it out and waited, tension mounting. He loosened his collar. Absurd to suffer all the physical symptoms of fear when whatever it was that was causing his distress was certainly not an ordinary landing on a perfectly clear day.

Then it came to him—his fear was a little like the fear of a lover who realizes that he is falling out of love. Had he really had any illusions about Poppy? Could anything about Poppy still take him by surprise? He would have said no when he got onto the plane, but then he would never have seen the image of a snake biting its own tail.

"No, no," he said aloud, to drive it away. He looked around quickly to see if anyone had noticed. For if the image was true—and Philip had an idea that this kind of image came from a deeper level than reasoning, and should always be explored—then it had something to tell him that he had better pay attention to. What was it? But even as he tried to decipher it, everything became vague and distressing again. He was suffering from claustrophobia, he supposed, but it had nothing to do with being shut up in a plane. It was, he realized, with a wave of nausea, quite simply that Poppy's freedom was his own prison. She and Reed had been his way out of his own uncertainties, a place of refuge, and now he saw that he was going to be locked up with himself.

Seeing anything clearly after the seizure of the last minutes was such a relief that Philip was able to be philosophical again. Do we always make our freedom out of someone else's bondage? he asked himself, as the pilot's voice came on again to announce a short delay. The passengers could smoke if they wished. Philip lit a cigarette and sat up. He felt a lot better and so was able to turn his thoughts toward Emerson. He had promised Reed to stop to see Emerson at his college in Illinois on the way home. "Tell him not to worry," Reed had said. "This is a temporary separation."

"Do you really believe that?" Philip had not been about to become the messenger of false hope, and, besides, he dreaded the whole idea of this errand. "Emerson and I don't really get on, you know. I doubt if he wants to see me." Philip never did get an answer about whether Reed could believe this whole nightmare would turn out to be just that, and not a reality. But he finally had agreed to see the boy and reassure him as far as possible. And he was taking him the jacket Emerson had asked for. At least that needed object might make him welcome, he supposed.

Of the three children, Emerson had always seemed the most balanced and the least troubled by his parents' squabbles. He was his father's boy and merely tolerated Poppy. So he had not agonized as the twins used to, and he had the best of Reed. They went off to ball games and on fishing expeditions together and he had thrived on being so obviously the favorite. But it didn't make him very appealing, Philip had to admit.

They were landing now. Philip was glad to be at the end of the journey and about to talk about purely practical matters with Chris. In the original design for the church there had been a bell tower, a round tower that Philip found quite beautiful. But, with building materials at such exorbitant prices, he supposed that would have to go. It had given the design its distinction—oh, hell!—was he so used to compromising that, as Poppy had often complained, he never put up a fight for his work? But how to be adamant with an old friend who simply did not have the money? Everything came back to human adjustments and compromises in the end.

Chapter V

Emerson was waiting on the dormitory steps when the taxi drove up, a slight, tense boy in a red shirt, and as Philip caught him for that second unaware he was touched by something vulnerable and wary about Emerson. He was frowning against the light, one hand in his jeans pocket, but the casual look seemed deliberately put on as a shield. Then he recognized Philip and came down stiffly to greet him.

"Hi. Here's your jacket."

"Thanks." Emerson slung it over his shoulder. "Don't know how I ever forgot it. I wear it all the time."

"I'll take you out for lunch if that's all right. Have to keep the cab anyway. We have only an hour."

Emerson suggested Howard Johnson's just down the road, no doubt because his idea of a meal was a milkshake and a cheeseburger, but also, Philip thought, because Howard Johnson's represents to those far away from home absolute security, the security that comes from knowing exactly what to expect in exactly what surroundings. Emerson was quietly observing Philip as they bounced along on a rough cement road, but neither of them felt like talking.

"Think Dad would give me a car? I sure would like to get out of here for a soda now and then."

Philip smiled. "A car for a soda might not strike your father as a necessity."

"But I could drive home for weekends."

"I'll ask him, Emerson. No harm in trying."

"Thanks."

The stiffness got worse when they were seated opposite each other in the booth, and had given their order. Human beings, like animals, Philip had often observed, cannot settle down while waiting for food. Emerson was clearly restless and ill at ease, talked with some enthusiasm about playing soccer, said he was now on the freshman team. Philip asked questions about his roommate and gathered that Firman was not a total loss. He was teaching Emerson to play chess, was not an athletic type, had come to college from a Chicago slum on a scholarship. Talking about Firman, Emerson smiled for the first time.

"He calls me a rich kid who has a lot to learn. I never thought about being rich before. Firman has only two pairs of socks and three shirts." The short declarative sentences poured out in a steady stream, as though a second's silence might be dangerous. Philip hadn't the foggiest idea how to approach the subject that lay between them like a locked box.

But at last food arrived. Emerson swallowed half his milkshake at one gulp, took up the cheeseburger, and mumbled, "I just can't understand why they have to do it," before he took a huge bite.

Philip watched him, eating and drinking with apparent total concentration, and found no word. After a time the silence got to Emerson and he raised his eyes, his father's blue eyes, and stared at Philip. "Do you understand it?"

"Not entirely. But people grow up, change. Your mother—"

"My mother is a mess."

It was so exactly like his father's way of reacting that Philip smiled.

"What's funny?"

"Nothing. You sound like your father."

"He's very upset."

"He's talked to you about it?"

"He calls me quite often at night. I wish he wouldn't."

"I can see it would be hard on you."

Mollified by the note of sympathy, perhaps, Emerson relaxed a little. "He thinks Mummie should see a psychiatrist. What do you think?"

"I think that might have helped her years ago."

"Too late now? Of course, she's awfully old."

Philip ate to keep from showing his anger, for he did feel revolted by the arrogance of this boy and his total lack of understanding or even wish to understand, apparently. But after a moment he forced himself to speak.

"Your mother has a volatile temperament, Emerson, but she is not, as far as I know, in need of that sort of help. There's nothing wrong with her except that she . . ." But here Philip hesitated, unable to find the words because he was really at a loss to explain Poppy to this hostile son.

"Except that she wants out after twenty-seven years. It's crazy!"

"So far you have heard your father's side—and naturally he's very upset. But there are always two sides, you know."

"Mummie wrote me a letter." He frowned. "May I have a chocolate sundae, please?"

"When I can catch the waitress' eye. Apparently your mother's letter did not illuminate matters."

"Oh, she talked about her art, wanting to be able to do it. She said she'd stayed so long for *our* sakes. That's what burns me up. It's all been a lie . . . for years . . ." Emerson's voice broke. He swallowed. The whole papier-mâché scene he had tried to make believable, the façade of not caring, had collapsed. Thank God, Philip thought, for at last we can talk.

"It's been an awful shock for me too. I feel as though my world had cracked in two. I find it almost as hard as you to accept."

"Accept what?"

"Accept that your mother has made up her mind and that nothing is going to change it. We have to cope with what is, not with what you or I wish were possible, not with what might be—if only. . . . The only way you can help your father, Emerson, is not to give him false hopes."

"You've always been on Mother's side, haven't you?"

"Have I?" Philip played for time, for there was a grain of truth in this accusation. "Maybe I have. But don't forget that Reed and I have always been very good friends—in fact, I think of him as my best friend."

"O.K. But you were probably in love with Mummie."

"Curiously enough, no," Philip said at once, wondering as he heard himself react so fast whether it was quite true, but also glad that Emerson could come out with this, once and for all, glad they could talk as two human beings at last. "Poppy and I see a lot of things the same way. We've always been perfectly congenial, but we have never been in love, Emerson. I can say that honestly." And he went on, thinking aloud, "No, the thing is that we enjoyed each other enormously as a threesome. I suppose that seems awfully queer, but we had a great deal of fun over the years. I can't believe it's over."

At last Philip caught the waitress' eye and ordered coffee for himself and a sundae for Emerson, who was playing with a fork and seemed not to be listening. Finally he said, "Harry and Susie are on Mother's side. They seem to think she's right to leave—as though my father were a leper."

"Even when there has been real love, people change, you know. Have you ever had a best friend some year and then another year couldn't care less?" Philip asked gently. "Human relations just are not fixed in their orbits like the planets—they're more like galaxies, changing all the time, exploding into light for years, then dying away. Feelings change as people change, and that's no crime."

"Marriage isn't friendship," Emerson said, granting perhaps that he had changed his mind about friends. "It's different."

"Yes, it is. But lasting marriages are also friendships."

"How do you know? You aren't married."

"Quite. But neither are you, and you seem to have some pretty definite ideas about it."

Emerson bent his head over the towering concoction the waitress put down, but, for once, did not start devouring it. He looked helpless and miserable. "Well," he mumbled after a considerable pause, "they're my parents, after all. When they quarreled it made me feel sick." The boy looked up straight at Philip, but as though he were not there. "It was worse when Mummie just kept away out in the studio and wouldn't talk."

"It may be better that they don't put each other through all that any more."

But Emerson had no answer for this and Philip suspected he was close to tears. It is a mistake to suppose that talking things over is always a help, Philip thought, and looked nervously at his watch. The time was running out.

"Why did you come to see me, anyway?"

"Reed asked me to."

"I suppose he wants me to come home for Thanksgiving."

"You'd rather not?"

"Well . . ." Emerson hesitated. "No. I mean, I'd rather stay here. Tell him we have soccer practice, will you? I just can't go back yet. It's not home anymore."

"I know how you feel. But Lucy comes in five days a week now, and everything looks very much the same. Your father and I have dinner together fairly often. He's absorbed in the new project at the factory, driving himself hard. He's very much himself, Emerson. Maybe you should come and see."

"Sometime—not yet." A cold, firm stance. Philip respected it. "I don't want to listen to all that garbage. Besides, I'd have to see my mother."

"I think maybe that's wise. I think we all have to have time to sort things out. Sorry to cut this short, but we'll have to move on if I'm to catch that plane." Philip was already on his feet. He knew he had failed to be of any help, and was himself raw with emotion. He and Emerson were not fellow sufferers; all they could do was exacerbate each other's pain. Probably Emerson was as relieved as he to have the session over. The boy insisted on walking part of the way to save Philip a detour back to campus. His last view of Emerson was a quick wave, then the slight figure walking slowly, kicking a pebble in front of him.

Well, it was clear enough that Emerson was bottling up too much, too much conflict around his mother. He was the one who could be helped now by a psychiatrist, by someone to whom he could talk it all out freely. But Reed would never admit the need, anymore than he would face that need in himself. For Reed, psychiatry was associated with failure, and it had really been out of contempt for Poppy that he had once wanted her to see a "shrink"—and because she had sensed this, she had never been willing to go.

Emerson was taking his father's way, choosing anger and hatred to avoid the pain of growth. But Emerson was young; what price would he pay if he came to terms with the divorce by hating his mother?

Philip felt wrung out. What he had suffered in the last hour came from seeing more clearly than ever before what Poppy had cost everyone close to her. Her lack of self-restraint imposed restraint on those around her; her violent changes of mood led to coldness in those who suffered from them. Loving, discerning, natural, dear as she was, this woman had aroused hatred in her youngest child.

But as he flew homeward Philip knew also that right now she was the one person he most wanted and wished to see. Instead, he had an appointment for lunch with Reed's mother the next day. He had managed to put her off for two weeks, but he had exhausted all excuses by now, and there was nothing for it but to face the music—a whole brass band, he thought with a shudder. Mrs. Whitelaw was a professional charmer who lived, Philip sometimes thought, a little above the ground, skimming the surface like an accomplished skater who chooses not to know that ice sometimes cracks and people on skates occasionally drown. Her whole relation with Reed had been false, a total lie, Philip thought now, amazed at the savagery with which he pounced on those words. But he was changing, he knew, changing in appalling ways. He, who had always considered himself tolerant and gentle, was becoming something quite different.

Cecilia Whitelaw should have been an actress, and might have been a great one. Instead, she had chosen to act her whole life out as though she were on a stage. Her longing for glory meant that she was always a little condescending to Reed, her only son, who should surely have been a diplomat or a financier, and instead ran a business. "How are things at the factory, dear?" she would ask with an air of mild amusement, as though a factory were as outrageous and amusing as having a love affair with someone not quite of one's own class.

The real trouble seemed to be that it was Cecilia herself who could have been a superb ambassador, or at the very least a magnificent hostess for an ambitious man. Instead, she had married a comfortable corporation lawyer, a gentle humorous man, "my true-blue David," as she described him herself. David had reached his ambition before he was forty—to make enough money to be able to retire in comfort and give his children a good education.

Reed had undoubtedly gotten his drive from his mother, whom he did not really like, Philip decided long ago, but whom he desperately wished to please. And Reed's tragedy had been that neither his ambitious mother nor his unambitious wife understood anything at all about his genius as a businessman, and each treated the factory with contempt. His father had been both proud of him and helpful with sound financial advice. But unfortunately David Whitelaw died soon after Reed was in litigation in which he played an inglorious part. He won the case eventually, against an inventor whose idea he had—if not stolen outright—borrowed. Then Reed had made the man a fairly large "gift" after the court case was settled.

"I suppose I gave Mr. Dana that ten thousand as a kind of debt to Dad," he had told Philip. "But he didn't approve. I knew that, though he was too sick then to say much." The last time Philip had ever seen him David Whitelaw had talked. The effort of speaking even those few sentences had seemed immense. "How can Reed equate justice with money? Do someone out of his rights and then square it away with money?" He had looked at Philip then as though he were trying to find words for something close to his heart. But he hadn't been able to. He had reached out a hand and Philip had risen to take it in his, never to forget the intensity of that handclasp. The force a dying man summoned to try to communicate a wish? What wish? The thing was finished, however badly. And surely David Whitelaw had known—he had worked with big business all his life—that one didn't succeed in business without at least once or twice behaving like a gangster.

And this, just this, Philip remembered with a pang, was what Poppy had finally understood and wanted no part of. Yet now she herself was demanding a generous settlement and could not understand why Reed—with some reason, after all—was being punitive. Was it really that almost no one was fully prepared to pay for his real life? Was that it? How much more complex and pitiful we all are than we can ever fully admit, Philip thought, not leaving himself out, as he was more and more aware that his disarray about the separation had a lot to do with his own feelings of deprivation as a result of it.

They had been above the clouds in the sunlight, and now, as the pilot made the approach, were suddenly immersed in fog, a dim white light, no visibility at all. Then suddenly earth rushed up at them—little houses, streets, cars, the river! Home again—a long drink, food, Perseus, and sleep. He had rarely been more tired.

Chapter VI

No man in his right mind could fail to enjoy meeting Mrs. Whitelaw for lunch, Philip thought, as he watched her walking down the street a few yards ahead of him, impeccably dressed in pale gray with a chiffon scarf tied at her throat and, almost alone among the women in town, wearing a delightful hat. She still had the long thin legs of a gazelle and walked carefully, holding herself erect. Philip deliberately stayed behind so he could look at her. Later he enjoyed the deference with which she was seated, for she was like an old royalty, taking attention for granted, turning on him now her cold, pale blue eyes (Emerson, he realized, had inherited them) and her social smile.

"No liquor for me, dear Philip. But of course you must have a cocktail. Order me tomato juice with a sliver of lemon." As she slipped off her white gloves, she spoke of the gentleness of the late September weather, interrupting herself to remember that it was also the season of hurricanes, the equinoctial storms, troubling to the psyche—and there paused, apparently lost in thought, though Philip knew it was all acting, acting a person lost in thought for his benefit.

"You are particularly elegant and beautiful today, Cecilia."

"Don't be ridiculous. I'm an ancient turtle, enjoying the last warm days."

Philip was meant to smile and did. But not for the right reason. He smiled because at times of crisis Cecilia survived by paying more than usual attention to what she would wear, by preparing herself in every possible way to play the part required by whatever tragedy was upon her. If she had been a passenger on the *Titanic* she would have gone down, no doubt, in long white gloves and an opera cloak, and with perfect courage.

After the amenities she pounced, looking Philip straight in the eye. "Why won't Reed come and have a talk with me?"

"You mentioned that he had been keeping his distance."

"I want to know what is happening. No one tells me anything."

"Reed is in a state of shock. He doesn't want to talk about it."

"Even to his friends? I always supposed that my son and I were friends."

Philip let that pass. "I expect he feels bruised enough not to want you to see the wounds. Besides"—Philip decided to be frank rather than flounder on—"he is furiously angry with Poppy. When he does talk, as he has to me, it is simply to rail against her. I doubt if you would enjoy such a scene. I hate it myself. So we take it out in angry games of tennis. Talking with Reed at the moment is simply nonproductive, Cecilia."

"Unfortunately, I can't play tennis," she said with heavy irony. "But I am Reed's mother and I have a right to know what is going on. Will you try to tell me, dear Philip, just what this is all about? I presume Poppy has fallen in love. Women of her age often do. But why separate? Why not a discreet love affair?"

"Dear Cecilia, you are very old-fashioned," Philip smiled across at her.

"Old-fashioned? I thought I was being ultramodern. My mother would turn in her grave at the idea of condoning a love affair."

"Yes, no doubt. But your daughter, if you had one, would say that she was divorcing for no man's sake, but in order to become herself."

"Preposterous! You don't mean it! You can't mean to tell me that Poppy is asking for a divorce for *no* reason?"

"She feels that her sculpture is a valid reason, and she thinks she can never be a serious artist as Reed's wife." As Philip uttered these words, speaking for Poppy, he saw for the first time that perhaps Poppy was wiser and braver than he had been willing to admit.

"Has she a talent? I had always assumed that she lacked the discipline that major talent requires to come to fruition. But surely, Philip, this is an absurd reason to abandon Reed and go her own way so late in life? I find it quite hard to believe!"

"Perhaps we had better order. You must be hungry

and I am ravenous. I had a long day yesterday out in Minneapolis—and, by the way, I stopped off on the way home to see Emerson."

"How is the darling child?"

"I'll tell you in a second. Dover sole all right? Or perhaps sweetbreads with mushrooms? That is quite good here. Oysters first?"

"That would be lovely, dear Philip—sweetbreads and oysters. You spoil me frightfully, of course. Spoil everyone. I know how good you have been to Poppy and Reed—a pillar of strength."

Philip laughed. "Well, hardly! I rather think it's the other way round. I've basked in their life for years, not they in mine."

"When I first met you when Reed was in college, I used to think you were rather frail—six feet two, but so thin—but I was wrong. You are very strong, Philip, aren't you?" He caught Cecilia's probing look before she could hide it under her dazzling smile, dazzling in a slightly frigid way because all her teeth were false. She put out her hand and squeezed his across the table. "It's not been easy for you, has it?"

"I do feel rather like a bridge attached neither to one side nor the other of a tumultuous river—suspended in space."

"Dear Philip, how little one takes in the whole of such miserable affairs and their repercussions! Until this moment I have hardly considered what a blow you have suffered yourself. Your best friends!"

"Let me tell you about Emerson." If there was one thing Philip was not going to do it was cry on Cecilia's shoulder. He ordered a second martini to go with the oysters and then fell into a silence, thinking about Cecilia, not Emerson.

"What are you thinking about?"

"I was thinking that crisis, even breakdown, tests human relations—that's obvious—but also that in a strange way we live most deeply at such times. And I was thinking that you yourself thrive upon crisis, and in a way it is your element."

"That's a two-edged compliment, I think, but I'll take the less cutting one." She brushed it aside now, drawing back from further exploration of herself, and asked again to hear about Emerson, her favorite among her three grandchildren, Philip had always thought, because he was so like Reed.

"Emerson is such an orderly person," she said. "He must be dreadfully upset by the disorder that has come upon the family."

"He's taking refuge in anger like his father. I felt that it might be helpful if he could have a talk with the college psychiatrist, blow off steam."

Cecilia's eyes opened wide, then narrowed, as she rearranged the chiffon bow at her throat. She was flushed, and it occurred to Philip that Cecilia reacted to talk of psychiatry much as Reed reacted to talk of money—it fussed her.

"Oh, do you think so? I'm afraid it would make him self-conscious or induce too much self-pity. Far better that he immerse himself in college life. He is crazy about soccer, Reed told me on the phone the other day."

Oysters and sweetbreads had arrived and been eaten, and still, Philip realized, they had only once talked of Poppy. Yet he felt sure that this meeting had been arranged by Cecilia for the express purpose of discussing her daughter-in-law.

"The point is," Philip answered after he had ordered coffee, "that if people bury anger, it can be damaging. Emerson won't come home for Thanksgiving because he doesn't want to see his mother." He was deliberately opening the door with that statement.

"Why should he want to see her? He feels betrayed—we all do."

Much to his astonishment Philip saw tears in the eyes of this highly controlled personage.

"Wasn't your first reaction anger, Philip? And do you intend to see a psychiatrist?"

"Of course not. But I'm grown-up and presumed to be able to handle my anger. At least it will not, as it might for Emerson, affect my relations with women . . ." But here Philip had to withdraw into silence, because as he uttered the words he understood that his anger had already affected his relations with Kathy. And that it was absurd to call himself grown-up.

He was roused out of reverie by Cecilia's incisive, "You'll have to discuss that with Reed." With that brusque statement she snapped off the thread. It was followed by an uncomfortable silence. Whenever this subject was discussed, the divorce itself, Philip thought, every road always ended in pain.

"I haven't been much help, have I?" What he wanted now was to get away, to get back to impersonal things, to the office. He signaled the waiter for the bill.

But Cecilia could not let it alone, now that she realized their time was running out. "Can't you talk to Poppy? Tell her she belongs at home, that it's too late for such radical change? For her own sake, I mean . . . what if she fails?"

"I think we have to admit that with all Poppy's faults she is a unique, valuable person. Somehow we have to trust her to know what she is doing."

"It's so mad. Where will she go? How will she live? There will be no frame, don't you see? How can a person just float around like . . . like a water lily without roots?"

"Ah, but Poppy would say that she had been rootless for years and that now the floating water lily will be rooted in hard work at an art."

"Why can't she work at her 'art' and stay with Reed? He's away all day, and he built her a splendid studio where she can lock herself up for hours if she chooses."

Now that they had got to the nub of things, Cecilia had become animated and—yes—almost real. The actress had left the stage and someone vulnerable and passionate was pleading with Philip. "Why does being 'a unique person' require so much self-indulgence, so little discipline, such tantrums, and such disregard for the feelings of others?"

Philip resisted the impulse to point out that people who are always thinking of the feelings of others can be very destructive because they are hiding so much from themselves. Instead, he followed the form he had chosen for this conversation—to act as Poppy's advocate.

"I expect Poppy would say that all that—the tantrums, the illnesses—sprang from the struggle of a human being trying to be born, or to be reborn after many years of being buried alive."

"No doubt that is what she would say, but can you condone it? No one forced her to marry Reed. I presume she was in love with him—and in every marriage the partners have to learn how to live together after *that* goes, surely."

Philip hesitated. Over and over again these days he was asked to take sides, to judge. No, he thought, I won't do it. "We are not asked to condone or to judge; we are asked to face a reality. It is as though Poppy had been suffering from an illness and saw a chance of recovery—the only chance—in making a fresh start alone."

"Do you believe that, Philip?" The glittering mask had gone and Cecilia looked her seventy-eight years. Philip was touched in spite of himself. There was something grand about this old woman, so framed by her life and her convictions, who yet insisted on pursuing the truth even when it broke the frame. She might be angry with Poppy, she might not understand Poppy, but she would still try to get at the harsh reality.

"Yes, I do believe it," he said after a second's pause. "Maybe your pushing me to the wall has forced me to see more clearly. I think Poppy tried very hard. All those attacks of colitis, those storms of tears and rage, were not self-indulgence. They were some deepest part of her rebelling against what her will was forcing her to do—to stay."

At this Cecilia gave a strange little laugh, the laugh as some last illusion cracks. "But why does personhood—if that is the modern word—always seem to involve ruthlessness about other people's personhood—Reed's in this case? What about Reed?"

"Reed is rather a ruthless man in some ways."

"Is he?" Again her eyes opened wide. "He's always been very gentle with me."

They were then to have it out, and Philip's idea of a quick escape had become impossible. "But he wasn't gentle with Harry about the war."

"Are we to be haunted by that war forever?" She visibly winced. "Harry is all right, isn't he? He got home safely."

"Maybe." Philip lit a cigarette. It was a tense moment. "As for that dirty war, yes, I think we'll be haunted by it forever."

"Why? There have been other wars . . . in my time two World Wars."

"Somehow we could always persuade ourselves that they were just. This war tore it all open—all the guilt we could handle and more. I guess what's left, what haunts, is the guilt we couldn't handle and haven't even begun to come to terms with." Philip felt such a storm of anger and pain rising in him again that he forced himself to change the tone. "You've put your hand in a hornet's nest, dear Cecilia—I'm sorry I'm so violent."

"I really want to know," Cecilia said quietly. "Please go on."

"About Harry. Unfortunately, what Reed did split the family up and down. And though Harry's experience in Vietnam did not end in disaster (how lucky for us all!), something that was firm in him when he wanted to be a C.O. has come apart. He's at a loose end. It's as if he didn't really care very much about anything, so he putters around. The latest thing is a printing press, I hear."

"I get the impression of a childish man doing exactly what he wants to do—he's so like his mother." But Cecilia caught herself at once. "I'm being unfair, of course. It's because it's so good to talk to someone at last, someone as fine and generous as you, Philip."

"I'm really a monster myself," Philip smiled. "I haven't been generous a bit, but I guess it's just rather more complex than we can fathom right away. Poppy was horrified by the war, and especially outraged by the Christmas bombing in '72, and she was obsessed by the defoliation of trees. She took it very hard, Cecilia, and that is surely to her credit. She cared very deeply, and little by little, after Watergate especially, she came to feel that fundamental dishonesty had been at work all through our culture—that it had seeped down even into personal relations. I suppose that in her characteristic wholehearted way she suddenly decided that each of us had to make a new beginning, to be more honest with ourselves than ever before, that this was, perhaps, the only way out of disintegration and decadence. I know it sounds absurd . . ." For in Cecilia's silence he sensed withdrawal. She simply could not follow Poppy here, and yet, even as he had tried to explain it, he saw clearly that this, just this, was the crux of the whole matter.

"I'm in the dark," Cecilia said. She looked drained.

Philip glanced at his watch. "I wish I could stay and talk forever, Cecilia. But I have an appointment at two and I'm afraid I have to run." Then he added quickly, "You have helped me understand by letting me talk."

"You are an angel to have given me all this time."

"Nonsense."

There was nothing more to say, after these "Japanese bows" of polite farewell had been spoken, and they made their way out.

"Is Reed all right?" Cecilia asked just before she got into a taxi he had signaled for her.

"He's handling himself well . . . working . . ."

The words floated off into the dusty air. The taxi door slammed and the last thing he saw was Cecilia's white-gloved hand waving.

Chapter VII

The talk with Cecilia had helped. Having to defend Poppy had clarified his own thoughts and Philip felt as though a fog had lifted. In a burst of euphoria he called Kathy that very afternoon and invited himself to dinner.

"Well, you're lucky it's my night off," she said. "And I have salmon—cooked it this morning. You might bring a bottle of wine."

It was a warm evening, so warm he had not even put on a jacket, but dashed off in sneakers, shorts, and a short-sleeved cotton shirt. And all the way through the traffic, across bridges, and up the river he was tremendously excited and so impatient to get to Kathy at last that he drove recklessly. Her apartment was on the third floor of a red-brick apartment house. He stupidly ran up and was panting when she opened her door.

"I'm out of breath."

"What's the hurry?"

"Oh," he flung himself down in the big blue chair

by the sofa, "I'm a fool. But suddenly I just couldn't wait to see you."

At this Kathy laughed. "Suddenly . . . after three weeks? You're nuts."

He looked up at her standing there so large and natural in a comfortable housecoat, and sighed.

"I know. I'm nuts. But I'm awfully glad to see you anyway." And now the distance between them became intolerable and he had to get up and take her in his arms, squeezing her hard against him in a warm hug. "Kathy," he murmured, kissing her ear before he let her go, "Kathy, what would I do without you?"

"You seem to have done very well without me lately."

"No, badly." He shook his head. "I've been feeling old and scared."

"You need a drink. Gin and tonic? I have limes."

"I'll make it."

While they got things together in the tiny kitchen, Philip was savoring the experience he had found here for ten years, the experience of feeling absolutely at ease and himself. They had done this many times before, teasing each other over small things like the bottle opener never being at hand, amicable and loving. Why was it so good here? Philip had never really found the answer. The apartment was nondescript except for an English highboy Kathy had inherited from her mother and two rather charming water colors of flowers that Philip had brought back from Paris once. But back in the living room with the drinks Philip looked around him in great contentment, while Kathy, still in the kitchen, was busy cutting a slab of sharp cheese into pieces.

"You're a handsome woman," he said when she came back. She had a round, strongly molded face, penetrating gray eyes, and a look of being in perfect command of herself and of being—how to say it?—very much a woman but with none of the usual affectations. He loved her plumpness, the innocent unsophisticated *embonpoint*. "Mmmm," he murmured, "you know, you're the best-looking woman I ever see."

"Thanks, chum. The only compliments I hear at the station are when some guy says I remind him of his mother!"

They laughed at that, laughed in the pleasure of being so old and so in love.

"Little do they know!" But as the laughter subsided, Philip sighed, thinking of age. "It's hard to realize one can't run up the stairs any more . . . and when I look in the mirror when I'm shaving, I'm appalled. Does anyone our age feel inside the way he or she looks outside?"

"A tall thin man like you never looks his age. I wouldn't worry." But she did look at him keenly then. "You look tired, Phil. That's what it is. It's not age you're suffering from. It's . . . What is it, anyway? That divorce? You look as though you'd been on a three-week binge," and very gently she leaned over and covered his eyes with her hand.

He kissed the palm as she withdrew it. "That felt good."

"The trouble is they all lean on you and not one of them has a clue as to what that takes out of you."

"Singular people like you and me are supposed to

have no problems of their own. Sometimes I feel like a sort of universal old sofa."

"Maybe you'd better get married," Kate teased.

"Thanks, old friend." This was a game they often played. It was a game because each knew the other was not the marrying kind. Kathy had had enough of marriage after her experience with an alcoholic husband and a divorce before she was thirty. "Marriages these days seem to me more and more to be cover-ups."

"How?"

"People marry because they are terrified of not getting married. Marriage covers up a lot of insecurity, looks in itself like 'success' of a kind, I suppose."

"I wonder. From what I see of the young these days, they're onto something else, better maybe, maybe worse. Of course, I run into the worst in my profession. But take the drugs away and they would make a lot of sense. They're way out nowhere and they're scared, Phil. I don't blame them." She sat as she often did with her hands clasped on her knees, her head thrown back. "Between the dirty war and the dirty politics, what have they got to stand on? No jobs around these days. But I'll say this for them—they know money isn't the answer."

"Unfortunately, money often is the answer. Money is still power, whatever they may think." Phil was thinking of Reed, convinced that he could use money as a lever to bring Poppy home.

"They're suspicious of power. They see it, I guess, as mostly bad."

"You mean used badly, I presume."

"Phil, it's good to talk again. That's the best thing about us . . . we can talk." Phil responded to the word "best" with a quizzical look, and Kathy chuckled. "All right, almost the best." She looked at her watch. "It's six-thirty. Do you want the news?"

"Of course." It wasn't only the news he wanted; it was sitting together on the couch, drinking quietly, spoofing the ads, talking to themselves as they watched the horrible world outside going about its business. This was peace. This was rest, Phil thought, as Cronkite's bland fatherly face came into view. He leaned over, took Kathy's hand, and held it on his knee.

"All right, my love?"

"Mmmm . . ." Phil laid his head back on the couch for a moment, feeling tension flow out of him, feeling as though he had been up in the air, circling, for days, and now at last had landed safely on earth.

Had Poppy and Reed ever known this kind of pleasure simply in being together? Thinking of them, he leaned forward and picked up his drink. Senator Sam Ervin was on the screen now, then Senator Weicker. More political garbage was being uncovered, and already the moment's peace was gone, blown away in gusts filled with old newspapers and specks of dirt by the prevailing winds.

"Make me another drink, dear," Kathy said in the next break. And she called out to him in the kitchen, "Are you hungry?"

"No, let's see it all—Chancellor—" For, Philip thought, we are so used to a climate of dirt and more dirt that it's become like a drug. We are suffering from a false hunger, not really a hunger for justice, simply a continual malaise, as though we had a perpetual hangover and had to have a powerful dose of the dog that bit us to keep going day by day.

"It only upsets you."

Phil patted Kathy's head after he had laid her drink down. "Yes, but I'm accustomed to my state," he sang to the tune of "I've Grown Accustomed to Your Face." He looked at the familiar room as though it were somewhere long ago. "Even here we can't really get away, can we?"

"Who wants to? It's our world," Kathy said matter-of-factly. "We live in it."

The screen was now showing the distraught faces of a couple whose house had been broken into and torn to pieces by Federal agents looking for a cache of heroin. The woman was clearly on the verge of breakdown. Her hands shook.

"Delightful country—the land of the free and the home of the brave!"

"I hate those Feds. They come in from the outside. They don't know the neighborhood. They haven't the foggiest idea what they are doing."

"I guess all that's left for us to believe in is personal relations—such as they are."

"What's wrong?"

"I didn't mean us."

"You were thinking about Reed and Poppy again. Phil, you're taking this too hard."

Philip turned off the T.V., got up, and walked over to the windows. Two boys were tossing a football back and forth down in the street. From another apartment he could hear a Chopin prelude being hesitantly picked out.

"It's eaten up all the vigor and vim I ever had."

"You'll feel better when it's settled."

"Maybe . . ."

"You haven't told me anything, really, except that Poppy left the house and wants a divorce. It happens every day, man. Every hour of every day some woman has had it and walks out. Is that a tragedy?" she asked his back.

"Not to you, evidently."

"Well, you don't have to be cross."

"I'm not cross. I'm just gutted."

At this Kathy laughed. "It's the first time I ever heard of a man being gutted by someone else's divorce! Listen, it's not *your* life!"

How could he explain that it had seemed to be his life and that that was the pang? He couldn't; instead, he came back to sit beside her. Kathy put an arm round his shoulder. "I've missed you, you son of a gun." He could feel her wondering about him, wondering how she could help, and after a moment she went on, "We've been through a lot in ten years—whatever is wrong, Phil, you know I love you, and you love me. That's not nothing."

"No, it's not nothing, Kathy."

But he felt dismally unable to respond, and his horrible fears about impotence flooded back.

"Well, then let's have some salmon and forget those people!" Then, as he didn't move, she added hesitantly, "Or do you want to talk about them?" They never had, or very rarely. Philip talked to Kathy about his work, but there had been an unspoken understanding that he came here as a free man, free of all that could not concern her. But of course Philip knew her well enough to be aware that she was ultrasensitive about his life. She wanted no part of it, she often said. Why drag it all out and spoil the evening?

"Yes, let's have some salmon! I'm ravenous!"

He helped Kathy set up the card table, found the cloth and silver, set out glasses, uncorked the bottle of Vouvray he had brought, and even as he did these familiar things, the moment of tension and panic passed. Soon they were laughing till tears rolled down their cheeks at one of Kathy's stories about a detective who dressed up as a woman and managed to look so grotesquely unconvincing that his own mother said, after one look at him, "If you're a woman, I'm Jesus Christ."

Later Philip told her about what he called "the disaster" in Minneapolis. The plans he had worked on so hard would now result in "a small holy barn," he said, because Chris couldn't afford the tower. And again they laughed the happy irrelevant laughter of people who have come through.

"A small holy barn indeed," and Kathy chuckled. "You know why you're such a darling?"

"Because I bungle everything?"

"No, because you don't take yourself seriously. You can always joke about the hard things."

"Poppy says I have no ambition. Maybe that's why."

Kathy frowned, got up, and took the plates out to the kitchen.

"Come back, I want to kiss you."

"Oh, heck," her voice came back from the kitchen, "the pie's burned."

"Who cares? Come here, woman. I want you."

An hour later they were stretched out, comfortably naked, in the big bed, Kathy reading aloud the first chapter of *Great Expectations*, while Philip rested his head on her soft belly, his eyes closed.

Every now and then she looked down at him to see whether he was asleep, then went on in her deep warm voice.

"Are you asleep?" she asked as she turned the page.

"No. Just dreaming . . ."

"You tickle me and I can't read properly."

"That better?" He had turned so his back lay against her thigh.

"Much better. Shall I go on? I'd forgotten how marvelous this chapter is. Remember when we first read it?"

"No."

"In that awful little cottage in Bermuda in the rain."

"It's better here than anywhere else," he murmured.

"We don't have much luck with journeys, do we?"

"No luck . . ." He felt sleep dragging him down in its undertow. Good old prick . . . it had given them both a lot of joy, after all. And then the lovely dark was there as Kathy turned off the light and gently pulled one of his ears before she turned over.

Chapter VIII

As Philip walked over to Reed's a few days later, leaves whirling around in warm wind and rain, the bittersweet, earthy smell of autumn in the air, he realized what an effort it was to see Reed at all. He had become Reed's whipping boy and it was damned uncomfortable. There was no point in arguing with the embattled, furious, unjust man, but keeping silent took its toll and after these sessions Philip felt physically battered. It had been a shock to hear, the last time, that Reed had purposely chosen a rock-ribbed Catholic lawyer and filled him with half-truths about Poppy's incompetence, selfishness, waywardness, and God knows what else.

Good thing for Poppy that the Massachusetts divorce laws had changed a bit for the better, though not much. But at least a fake scene of violence would not have to be set up as had been the case twenty years ago when Philip had been a witness in the divorce of a friend of his. That had been an ugly business and he winced, remembering it. For the fake scene that had been arranged so that Philip and another friend could testify in court without perjuring themselves had been changed in the playing of it to a horribly painful moment of truth, when Claire after the pretend-slap ran out into the hall and fell to her knees, sobbing and beating her head against the banisters in an attack of hysterical grief.

Philip had not, technically speaking, perjured himself, but he knew in his heart that he had lied to the judge because there had been no violence in the marriage; it was simply that Hugo wanted a divorce. It was not a good memory to take with him into Reed's house that evening.

"I'm in here," Reed called out from the library as he heard the door open.

Philip took off his wet raincoat and went in to find Reed sitting behind the desk wearing his black horn-rimmed glasses, a ruffled owl glowering at a pile of papers and canceled checks. The room had the stale smell of cigars. There were no flowers. It had begun to look, Philip felt, as impersonal and cold as a hotel room.

"You should tell Lucy to pick some chrysanthemums. It looks sad with no flowers in here."

"That was my wife's job. Lucy is not my wife."

"Is arranging flowers a marital duty? For God's sake, Reed, you might as well be living in a hotel."

"Most men couldn't care less about flowers. I don't know why you do."

Philip laughed. There was nothing else to do. You couldn't win when Reed was in this mood. "I'd pick some for you myself, but it's too wet out."

"If you're so hell-bent on making yourself useful,

you might mix us a drink. I'll come out on the porch in a minute—all I do in here is accounts."

"What's for dinner?"

"Lucy left a casserole, I think."

"I'll make a salad."

"Whatever you like."

Dismal atmosphere! There was no real lettuce, just iceberg, and brown at the edges, at that. He did find a few tomatoes, but no onion in the refrigerator. Really, Philip thought, Susie and Harry should come over and humanize things. Lucy could obviously use some suggestions about menus, and no doubt also a little moral support. But would Susie and Harry be willing? Philip had no idea what their relation to Reed was now. There was a lot he didn't know, though his life was being consumed in finding out, in being told, in listening. Not my life, *their* life, he said to himself. I'm caught up in a relentless machine of other people's feelings.

"Hey, where are the drinks?" Reed was standing in the doorway.

"Sorry. I was making a salad—out of rather poor materials, I must say."

"Oh, very well, I'll mix the drinks. Martini all right?"

Philip stood against the counter and watched Reed measure the vermouth and gin, admiring the precise way he did things, even when he was as tense and irritable as he was tonight.

"You are a bit prickly this evening."

"Sorry, Phil. It's good of you to come."

"Not at all. A pleasure."

Reed lifted his head and shook himself like a dog

shaking off water. "Brrr . . ." he said. Then they laughed, and the spell of bad humor was broken. "The thing is, Phil, I don't like myself and I don't like anyone else very much these days."

"The whole human race is rather a mess, let's face it."

"Come on out."

They took their drinks out to the porch. Philip looked out at the steady rain pouring down, then took a sip of his martini and set it down. Reed was sitting, hunched over, and had not touched his. And Philip waited. He was not going to stick his neck out this time.

"Thanks for seeing my mother," Reed said without enthusiasm.

"I always enjoy Cecilia. She's so serene and above the melee."

"Really? I don't think so. She calls me nearly every day, probing, wanting to know, extending comfort and the usual barbs. Damn it, Phil, why can't she leave me alone?"

"It's fairly natural. She *is* your mother."

"She even offered to come over here with the faithful Emma and take care of me for a while. Imagine! As if it weren't enough to have my wife run away without having my mother move in!"

Philip chuckled. "What did you say?"

"I don't remember. I think I slammed the receiver down. My nerves are shot, Phil. I'm not myself."

"How are things at the factory?" Philip asked, trying to get onto a more congenial subject.

"All right so far. There are all sorts of rumors about shortages. I'm stock-piling. And that means a lot of figuring. We may have to build a bubble for extra space. But costs are astronomical, as you know, even for that sort of structure."

"Yup—and they won't come down, from what I hear."

"How about you? Did your friend think they could manage the round tower?"

The minute Reed talked about the business he was his old self. They hadn't talked shop for ages, not since Poppy's letter. But inevitably telling about Philip's trip came round to Emerson and they were back in the painful private present. Reed scotched any idea of psychiatry for the boy with a short "I can't afford it."

"Emerson will be all right, but I'm afraid if he has to handle this alone he'll handle it by hardening, and that could affect his life later on."

"Let him. He'll have learned his lesson about women like Poppy and find somebody who can keep house and keep her temper when his time comes."

"When his time comes there may not be any such women around."

Reed frowned. "If you can believe it, I'm being hounded by the FEPC to hire more women. Not secretarial. I mean at benches in the factory!"

"Well, it might not be a bad idea at that. In World War II women did a lot of that sort of thing you remember. They're good at pernickety work."

"They're a pain in the neck, always taking sick leave. Besides, the men won't like it. They want their own shop."

"Yes," Philip said, half-amused, half-sad, "I expect so."

"I feel like a dinosaur!" Reed burst out. He stood and paced up and down, rumpling his hair, and Philip couldn't help laughing, remembering what Harry had said not long ago: "My old man has the instincts of a prehistoric animal."

"What's funny?"

"Nothing."

"Then why did you laugh?"

"Oh, I don't know—your violence, the way you react. Isn't it better to take it humorously?"

Reed flung himself down again. "What am I going to do, Phil? How am I going to handle all this anger?" He groaned, a groan of such real distress that Philip was touched.

"I guess one just lives through it like an illness. I'm angry too all the time," he added, "if you must know."

"What have you got to be angry about? Nobody walks out on you. They all flock around you. I suppose you've seen Poppy?"

Philip chose to ignore the second question. "I'm angry and I have no reason to be, just as you say. That doesn't make it any easier."

"What did Poppy say?"

Philip took a deep breath, then looked Reed in the eye with as much cool as he could muster. "It wouldn't be productive or honorable for me to run from one person to another telling tales. The only way I can keep my sanity is to be trustworthy. I'm not going to tell you what anyone has said, and that's that." But under the cool Philip knew dread. He had stated a truth he was sure to betray sooner or later. And a truth that was bound to enrage Reed.

"I'm to be kept in the dark, is that it? While you run around picking up the dirt on me, I suppose."

"Come on, man, this is not a good idea." It was Philip's turn to get up. He went out to the kitchen to make himself another drink.

Reed followed him. "I want you to tell Poppy something. She's not going to get what she wants."

"Do you know what she wants? I don't."

"She wants a generous allowance, enough to live on without taking a job. You read the letter."

"It's a matter for the lawyers, and I'm not going to discuss it."

For a second they faced each other like two boxers, wary, rigid with the effort to control an attack that might have come from either of them, but the tension was broken when Philip put down his glass, put his hands on Reed's shoulders, and forced Reed's eyes to meet his.

"We're friends, remember?"

"All right." Reed shook his head, made a half gesture toward Philip, and let his hand drop. "I'm shot to hell," he murmured as they went back to the porch.

The man was close to tears and Philip was shocked to see it, shocked out of his own irritation, shocked into paying attention as one does for a friend in need. It was startling to realize that this had not been possible before.

"I guess we all are."

"Not you, surely! Not you, old omniscience!" Reed had got hold of himself, since he could tease, Philip thought, and that made it possible to talk quietly out of his own dismay.

"It's hellishly hard for old middle-aged people to have to adjust to an earthquake. Reed, it's an earthquake for me too. You and Poppy have been the best friends I ever had. We had fun together. We were all set for another twenty years of banter, tennis, drinking, travel, good food, an occasional intellectual battle . . ." But as he heard the words fall into the air, heard them *after* they were spoken, he caught his breath. "That's it!" he shouted. "Eureka!"

"What is it, man? What's got you all of a sudden?"

"Don't you see? It was not real."

"What's so unreal about playing tennis, or cooking, for that matter, or good talk? Or being friends?"

But Philip was at a loss to explain what had come to him in a flash like revelation. He sat there, slouched in his chair, trying to get hold of whatever it was he now knew in his bones, but was not yet able to formulate in words.

"I can't tell you. But I think I understand Poppy for the first time."

"I wish I could get into your mind then, for I don't. I find Poppy's ethos childish and sentimental."

"In some ways it is. She hasn't given up hoping that life can and should be lived on a deeper level than any of us have tried. You and I accepted long ago that most of what we hope for is childish, and so we settled for whatever we have around without trying very hard."

At last Philip sensed that he had got Reed's attention, had got through the wall of anger.

"Go on," Reed said, and, when Philip didn't answer immediately, he himself volunteered, "You see, all that you call 'not real' is what you and I have fun with *after* work hours. My real life, I suppose, is at the factory. What I need when I come home is peace and quiet."

"Maybe Poppy resented that. Maybe she wanted to be part of your real life."

"How could she be? She wasn't interested, in the first place, and, in the second place, she was supposed to be having *her* real life in that studio I spent twenty thousand to provide."

"Yes, I know."

"Why couldn't she do it? What in hell prevented her from being an artist? Why does she have to leave her home and her husband and live in some cheap hotel to do it?"

"That is the question, isn't it? I wish I knew the answer."

"But you obviously have some clue. You must have, or you wouldn't have shouted, 'Eureka!' just now."

Philip had wanted to be able to talk, but now he was the one to hesitate, terrified of touching the raw wound. "Maybe Poppy wants to be whole—to bring together work and fun, as you call it, into a whole life."

"Where did I fail her, Phil? Please try to tell me." It was said quietly, with force, Reed at his most human and appealing. But how to answer? Things dimly perceived, never defined, crowded into his head—the idea that Reed had, consciously or not, broken some human compact more than once in the marriage—and once, quite certainly, by the way he handled his son over Vietnam.

"You're afraid of hurting me."

"Yes." And Philip added defensively, "Besides, I'm not God. How can I tell *you* what went wrong? I'm not inside your marriage."

At this Reed grunted. "You were close to it."

"Yes, I was. I've thought about that a lot lately. Maybe it wasn't good that Poppy could talk to me as she did, that you could talk to me as you did—I became a buffer state that prevented you from ever confronting each other."

"Wow! How can you say that?" Reed set down his glass and sat up straight. "The last ten years have been outright war half the time."

"It wasn't exactly peace and quiet."

"It was hell."

"Then why do you mind separating? Who wants to live in hell?"

Reed scratched his head and looked honestly bewildered. "I suppose I thought Poppy would quiet down as we got older. It wasn't all bad—we made the garden together."

"Yes, that was a real creation."

"I can't even go out there now and pick off dead heads. It makes me ill."

Philip was on the brink of offering to come and help with the autumn chores, when he stopped just in time. He was not going to take on the role of a substitute wife.

"I want my wife," Reed said loudly, "God damn it!"

"Well, she doesn't want you. It's hard, Reed, but you've simply got to accept that as a fact."

"All right," Reed growled, "why doesn't she want

me? What's wrong with me? That's what I want to know."

It had taken courage for Philip to make the harsh statement he had just laid on the line, and his instinct was to beg off. But one look at Reed's face, at the blank openness of it, a little like the wide-eyed, open look of a small bull, made him try.

"It could be simply that Poppy has been growing in her own strange way, and that growing has brought her into another country than marriage . . . So maybe it's not that there's something wrong with you at all. Poppy is changing—it's almost as though she were a giant moth who needs to make its cocoon. She's really interested only in herself at this point."

"Moth be damned!" Reed laughed his angry laugh. "It's absurd for a middle-aged, stout woman to emulate Narcissus, isn't it?"

"Maybe narcissism is implicit in the artist," Philip ventured.

"I hope she falls in the pool and drowns!" Reed laughed loudly again.

However dangerous this conversation, it was perhaps the first chance they had had to talk sanely, to think things out, and Philip couldn't leave it at that.

"Reed, has it occurred to you," he asked gently, "that you are mostly interested in *yourself?* Have you made much effort to take anyone else in lately?"

"Sure, I'm absorbed in what I'm doing. I'd be a pretty poor provider if I weren't. You know the risks I've taken, Phil. I've had a lot on my mind."

"And that seems to you perfectly natural."

"Of course. You can't run a factory in a semirecession and not put all you've got into it. I wake up at three in the morning, sweating it out."

Then Reed heard what Philip was really saying. Philip could see the words landing, as it were. "Besides, the factory is outside me. I don't spend hours looking at my navel, for God's sake. What is this, anyway?"

"It's hard to put into words."

"I can't see that it's monstrous to expect a wife to run the house and look out for the children, while one runs the business that provides the money."

"What if you were expected to run the business *and* run the house?"

"I wouldn't have time—or the skill, for that matter. No one taught me to cook."

"No, I don't expect that idea ever occurred to your mother!" They exchanged a humorous look over that. "Maybe Poppy feels that she can't do her work and run the house. Maybe it's as simple as that."

"Oh, come off it, Phil! What is her work?"

"Maybe she only senses what it has not been, and what it could be."

"But when a woman marries, she takes on a job. A marriage is two people working as a team. All this is certainly raising questions I wouldn't have thought needed answering, the answers are so obvious."

"The times are changing, Reed."

"Where have I been?"

"You haven't been paying a great deal of attention to Poppy."

"I gave her a diamond bracelet for her birthday. I'm still in love with her and I've proved it a hundred times."

Philip sighed.

"Doesn't she want to be treated like a woman? What proof of love does she need?"

"Whatever it is that makes a woman a person first, a human being in her own right, not an appendage of your needs, your need to show off by giving her an expensive jewel." For once Philip had let down his guard.

"That's enough!" Reed shouted. "I've taken all I'm going to take. Lay off!"

"I'm sorry."

"No, you're not. You sit there like God, telling me off." Reed banged his glass on the table.

"I wouldn't be here at all if I didn't care. You know that."

"I suppose so."

Philip got up. It was time to go. They were again on the border of dangerous irritation with each other.

"If you care, will you do one thing for me?"

"Anything, Reed."

"Be here when Poppy comes day after tomorrow to decide what things in the studio she wants crated and taken away. I want to see her, but not alone."

"Why not? That might be a good idea."

"I'm afraid I'd kill her." It was said quietly, but Philip knew it was true.

"I'll come if you promise not to wrangle."

"I can't promise anything—but I'll try."

"Take it easy, Reed," Philip said at the door. He realized suddenly that they had forgotten to eat. Too late now. He shrugged into his raincoat and went out into the rain.

Chapter IX

Harry lay on the floor with Perseus stretched between his long legs, while Susie carried out the dessert dishes, and in that pause that had come so naturally after all the talk, Philip basked in the comfort it was to be with the twins, to listen to Harry's plans to print single sheets of his friends' poems and sell them for a dime apiece, to hear Susie on the excitement of being a first-grade teacher—to enjoy civilized conversation for a change and to get away from the obsession.

Philip found he was looking at them differently and more understandingly than he could have done a few weeks before. Harry had the air of a lazy lion and had grown a little heavier, but the weight suited him—he had been terribly gaunt when he got back from the war. Susie was quick and active, as always, a tall boyish girl, with her hair tied back in a bow at the nape of her neck. Dressed alike in jeans and plain blue Chinese jackets, they looked a little like Watteau's *Gilles*, seen double. The thought amused

Philip because, having caught the image, he saw that it was exact. They did have something of the *Gilles's* intense, yet dreamy look, these two, and he smiled as Susie came back with coffee and filled his cup.

"Thanks, angel."

Harry picked Perseus up and laid him in the armchair, and then shifted around to sit up, cross-legged. Philip felt that he was being closely observed.

"If I were you, I'd go to London for a month . . . take off . . . You're tired out, Uncle Phil."

"Yes," Susie called out from the kitchen, "that's a great idea!"

"Do you two ever disagree?" Philip parried, for his first thought had been "I couldn't possibly!" Yet he could discover no rationale for this belief that he had to be part of the divorce as he had been part of the marriage, that running away would be cowardly and indecent.

"Of course we disagree. We have knock-down arguments about nearly everything," Harry said happily.

"At least about jelly on peanut-butter sandwiches!" Susie said, settling down on the big sofa.

"I couldn't leave Reed just now. I guess I'm the only person he can blow off to."

"He's got you mesmerized just the way he did Mother—it's always *his* needs that have to be met."

"Harry, Reed's my best friend. I can't walk out on him when he's up against something as shattering as this divorce. You have to remember that it hit him out of the blue; he was totally unprepared."

"The more fool he!" Harry said lightly.

"You're not quite fair, Harry," Susie said quietly.

"But if he thinks his marriage was happy, he's a fool—you have to admit that!"

Susie leaned back against the sofa, her eyes closed. She was not, Philip felt, going to allow herself to get into an argument. But Philip, in his mellow mood, felt like talking. "One of the things I've been wondering for two weeks is whether all marriages don't have the seeds of dissolution in them. Can people be expected to keep on growing at the same rate?"

It was Susie who answered. "I think it's more that men do their growing outside the marriage, most of the time, and women maybe inside the marriage. Even though Mother tried to have her own thing going too, she felt pinned down . . ." And she added, "She never felt really free, did she? She always felt guilty because she was not doing something else, like giving a cocktail party."

"Besides, what do you mean about men growing outside the marriage?" Harry asked.

"I don't know . . . maybe just that Pop's deepest challenge was his job. What do you think, Uncle Phil?"

"He had some pretty hard tussles and came out on top. Maybe he had to get harder and tougher to survive."

"Exactly . . . and as he got harder and tougher, he went way outside Mother's orbit. She didn't have a clue, really, did she?"

"We don't know, Harry. How can we *know?*" Susie asked plaintively.

"Reed thinks you've been brainwashed by your mother, you know."

"Shit," Harry said matter-of-factly.

"We're on Mother's side, but that doesn't mean we've been brainwashed." Susie was pink with indignation. "Pop's like a child, always blaming someone else."

"But," Philip intervened, "Emerson is on your father's side, and are *you* not going to say that *he* has been brainwashed?"

Susie laughed. "Well, I guess I might, at that!"

Harry turned to Philip, quite serious now. "Even in families there are affinities, real ones. Pop and Emerson hit it off. We never have. So it's not exactly taking sides, in my view; it's the way we are. Nobody's fault, just a kind of chemical mixture that works in Emerson's case and doesn't in ours. Emerson is rigid and Pop might as well be a dinosaur. They match up."

"What I want to know," Susie said, turning to Philip, "is what he was like when they met?"

Philip laughed. "Well, you'll find it hard to believe, but at M.I.T. Reed and I and some other fellas were called the Red Guard. I know, it does sound preposterous. What you seem to me to leave out, you two, is what responsibility does to harden attitudes, or groove them. Reed would say that is learning to face reality."

"And Mother would say that's compromise," Harry shot back.

"But she could afford not to be responsible. She had someone to support her, to be tough for her, if you will."

"Anyone can earn a living."

Susie frowned. "I don't know, Harry. We have had an easy time."

"In *some* ways. You are talking about money. Those are Pop's values. Having money enough is everything—that's all he cares about. That's all that matters."

Philip could not let that pass. "You know the factory is not just a money-maker. It's far more interesting than that. Those little gadgets he makes go into every rocket, into sophisticated computers, into a hell of a lot of things that help push the frontiers back, that are opening up the universe. Your father, in his way, has created something." For once Philip knew he was right in defending Reed, and he spoke vehemently because it was good to be able to.

"He hasn't done much inventing lately, has he?" Harry asked. "Isn't he mostly cashing in on an invention made in World War II?"

"Not quite so long ago as that."

"What does he put his mind on these days? Labor troubles, marketing, cursing the government!" Harry lay back against the chair, his hands behind his head. "He's furious at having to hire women!"

"Yes, we had a little argument about that the other night."

Susie slipped down to the floor and leaned against Harry's shoulder. "You can talk to him, Uncle Phil. We can't."

"You should have heard what he said when he saw the bill for the press . . . Mother had told me to go ahead."

Susie sat up. "But why didn't you ask me for the money, Harry?"

"I wouldn't borrow from you, Susie, for Christ's sake!"

"Yet," Philip said, seeing suddenly why this lazy, *laissez-faire* young man induced rage in his father, "you are willing to take it from your father, whose values you question."

As though he sensed what Philip was thinking, Harry lay back with exaggerated indifference. "Why not get what I can?"

"But that's exactly what Pop would say about some deal of his!" Susie said tensely. "Phil's right." And she got up and went back to the sofa.

"I'm perfectly willing to soak the rich," Harry said, unperturbed.

The bland self-assurance was irritating. But how to tackle it?

"I'm all mixed up." Susie punched a pillow with a sudden gesture of frustration and anger.

"The point is that soaking anyone, rich or poor, seems not a good idea . . ." Philip kept his tone mild, but he too was angry.

"Mother is out to get all she can out of Pop. Do you think she's wrong?" Harry, still smiling, asked.

"Money is such a troubling thing," Susie said. "I hate it."

"After all, money is power," Philip said, "and like any other source of energy can be used well or badly."

"Yes, but having it gives one an unfair advantage. People with money beat other people down in a thousand subtle little ways," Harry said.

"Not *all* people with money, surely," Philip answered.

Now Harry, interested, pulled himself up to sit beside his twin. "It's not always conscious, but in my experience they always do. It's a little like rank in the army. You can't beat rank and you can't beat money. Look at Pop! He can punish Mother by not giving her a decent settlement, and that's what he intends to do."

"Well," Philip said quietly, holding onto himself, "she had the power to punish him and has used it by walking out. Good God, Harry, if you are talking about *punishment!*"

"Don't be upset, Uncle Phil," Susie said quickly. "We can talk to you. You see, you are the only person."

"Everyone says that!" Philip got up, as though to break his sense of frustration by walking up and down, but then abruptly sat down again. "Pay no attention. I'm on edge."

"But you must understand why Mother had to do it. Please say you do," Susie pleaded.

"I don't know what I think."

"Let the man alone," Harry intervened. "We didn't mean to push you to the wall, Uncle Phil. I'm sorry." Then he added, rubbing his forehead, "I am disgustingly detached, but I guess that was the price of survival for me—and it goes back a long way."

Philip caught the anxious glance the twins exchanged, and made himself relax. He lit a cigarette. Then he said, smiling at Susie, "I really need to talk as much as you do." He inhaled deeply, set the cigarette down, and leaned forward, "It's been tense for me. I have been walking one tightrope after another, trying to keep my balance—your grandmothers—Emerson." And then he got up and walked up and down, thinking aloud, "But that isn't really the point. I am slowly coming to realize that your mother is making all of us face things we've tried to avoid facing for years. That's why it has been so painful." Neither of the twins spoke, but he knew as he stood, back to the room, looking out the window, how attentively they were listening. "Besides, when the boy takes his finger out of the dike, there's a flood. I've been that boy." And he turned back to them and laughed. "How presumptuous can you get?"

Harry nodded. "You held things together—now you can't any more. There is no dike. It's all been washed away."

"It's awfully hard for you, Uncle Phil, isn't it?" Susie had moved over to sit on the arm of Perseus' chair, close to her twin.

"It's lonely." But, having said so much, Philip withdrew. He had done enough crying on the shoulders of the twins, he told himself, and he shifted deliberately to a subject he had been pondering. "Poppy talks about Watergate, and the war too, as though her act of violent separation from the personal past stemmed from them . . . as though . . ." And he ended abruptly, "It seems such a feminine point of view."

"Don't do it, Uncle Phil!" Susie said with unexpected violence. "Don't!"

"Don't do what? What am I doing?"

"Making it 'feminine' to take a position like that, instead of simply '*human.*' It's human to try to fight your way out of corruption and despair!"

Philip, brought up short, chuckled. "Old-fashioned

as blackstrap molasses, aren't I? How can I say what I mean? These things, a marriage and Watergate, seem to me to be in different universes of discourse and to mix them up seems a little crazy." At least he had avoided saying, "Men separate these categories." And he added, feeling their eyes, piercingly attentive, " 'Corruption and despair' are strong words to apply to that marriage."

"It's not that." Susie frowned, "Harry, try to tell him."

"During the war there were no visible signs of corruption and despair at home, except for a few zany pacifists like me before I got drafted. But I'm sure, way down deep inside, people felt troubled. You couldn't look at those film clips of indiscriminate bombing, of children napalmed—not to mention My Lai—and not react."

"I'm a cynic, Harry. I'm afraid a lot of people didn't react at all."

"Of course. They had been so corrupted and brainwashed that they had lost some if not all of their true humanity. It *was* a corrupting war," Susie said, "you have to agree, Uncle Phil."

"I do agree. What I can't see is the intimate connection between that and your parents' divorce. That does seem farfetched." But as soon as Philip had said those words he saw how wrong he was and quickly added, "Of course, Reed was awful about Harry, and I suppose that may have had something to do with Poppy's decision."

"Let's not go back over that," Harry said firmly. "I think what Mother came to see was that Pop failed or compromised whenever he was in a tight spot. He lied to *himself*, just as Nixon does all the time. That's where she made the connection."

"You've shifted to Watergate, but I think I do see. Still I have to ask, 'Why leave your husband because the world is in a mess?' Nobody's perfect, is he?"

"It doesn't sound logical, does it, Harry?" Susie asked, smiling now. "But in some queer way it is. It is to us, I mean— and to Mother."

"She wouldn't have minded so much if she hadn't loved him," Harry said. "But when they argued she always was defeated or felt she was battering at a wall, and when she didn't argue, she got sick. How can you work at something if everything you believe in is undermined all the time by the person you live with?"

"Yes, I see . . ." Philip went on thinking and he had to utter his thought, once and for all, in the face of the absolutism of the young. "But I am not wholly on Poppy's side. I think compromise is very painful, but a peaceful settlement of war, whether intimate or public, involves both parties and their being willing to make concessions. A person who chooses to live outside this universal law risks creating anarchy or disaster."

"Maybe that's what we *have* to risk." Harry's hands were clasped round his knees; he rocked gently back and forth. In the last few minutes his detachment had fallen away. "I think Mother's got a lot of guts to do what she's doing. Who knows whether she can make it as an artist? She's old to make a start, a serious start."

"She will have enough to live on, won't she, Uncle Phil?" Susie asked.

"What does it matter?" Harry said quite crossly. "Mother isn't interested in things like cars, swimming pools, comfort—she never has been."

Philip suppressed a smile. "She'll have a lot to learn about doing without those despised things that come in so handy. No, I am thinking of more radical losses . . . loneliness . . ."

"Mother's such a vivid person, she won't be lonely!" Susie interrupted with absolute conviction. "Besides," she added with an affectionate smile, "she has you."

"I wonder whether someone who has been the friend within a marriage survives its dissolution. Hey!" Philip looked up, frowning. "I didn't expect to say or think that."

"You can't really help, you know. I do think you ought to go away for a month. Get right out and breathe your own air for a change," Harry said firmly.

Was it only that the young had learned to be ruthless these days, Philip asked himself, or was it that Harry, whatever his flaws of self-content, had achieved wisdom? Whatever it was, his tone and what he had said with such conviction were persuasive—London, Philip thought, and perhaps a long ramble through the Dordogne. "You've been a great help, you two," he said then, and got up again to walk up and down a moment.

The twins glanced at each other. "We'll just wash the dishes," Susie kissed Philip lightly, "and then leave you in peace. Come on, you lug," she said to Harry. "I'll need your help."

Listening to their laughter in the kitchen, Philip gave a long sigh and sat down again, at peace with himself for the first time in weeks. Whatever the pain and frustration in the union of Poppy and Reed, that difficult marriage had created these two, and once more one had to wonder whether this trust, this serenity, this curious lightheartedness could have been created without conflict and pain as its only true begetter.

Chapter X

Shortly after the twins had gone, leaving the kitchen immaculate, Poppy called Philip to ask whether she could pick him up on her way to the studio the next afternoon. The query was upsetting and Philip hesitated a second before answering, "I think we had better go separately, Poppy."

"But I can't walk in there alone and risk meeting Reed before you get there, don't you see?"

"I'll be ten minutes early. I promise."

"And then I walk in and find you and Reed together."

The voice was cold. Was he going to be forced at last to take sides? Was it impossible to remain the friend of both Reed and Poppy? Was this last comfort to be taken from him—the comfort of remaining true to what they had allowed to break down?

"Are you there, Philip?"

"Sorry. I was thinking."

"Well, if you're going to make such a thing of it, never mind. I thought you were my friend."

"I'm Reed's friend too."

"I don't see how you can be." Poppy was vehement now. "He's humiliated me in every possible way. My lawyer says he's never had to deal with a lawyer as adamant and uncomprehending as this O'Neil appears to be. Reed is out for blood."

Standing in the hall with the phone in his hand, Philip felt acute pain. Gently, stealthily almost, he put the receiver down and fled into the chill autumn garden in the dark.

He would have to call Poppy back, but at least he could give himself five minutes to consider. It was always some apparently tiny incident that brought on the crucial moments in human intercourse—that he had always known. But he was totally unprepared for this decision. He had held it at bay until now and he hated Poppy for forcing the issue. It wasn't fair. I'm a person myself, he thought, not a pawn in their game for power. I won't take sides.

The autumn smell—dank leaves, the bitter scent of chrysanthemums—penetrated his consciousness. There was no exhilaration in the fall this year. He hadn't even ordered tulips to plant. It felt like the end, and in three weeks he had aged ten years. "I'm an old man," he said to the trees. "Old and tired." But Philip caught the theatrical note and laughed at himself, and on that went in and made himself call Poppy.

"Sorry I hung up. I felt dizzy. Why don't you come over here and talk? The telephone is impossible."

"All right, I will."

While he waited, Philip emptied the ashtrays and went down to the cellar for logs. If he had felt slack and exhausted a few moments ago, he was now curiously excited and nerved up. In three weeks he had seen Poppy only once, and he realized how much he had missed her as he set out brandy glasses and a bottle of Courvoisier. Then he looked around the room critically, seeing it with Poppy's eyes—she would enjoy that bunch of deep orange chrysanthemums, nasturtiums, and white asters. It occurred to him that the twins had not noticed them. Flowers do not delight the young, not often. He was eager to tell Poppy about the twins. In fact, his mind raced from one thing to another, and if he had felt ten years older in the garden, he now felt ten years younger. At last he heard the car swing into the drive and the door slam.

"Well, damn it, I'm glad to see you!" he called out as she came up the path.

"Sh!" She put a finger to her lips and whispered, "Wait till we're inside."

"What's all this about?" He closed the door behind her.

"I think I'm being followed. Listen!"

Sure enough, they could hear a car gently coming to a stop. Philip put on the outdoor lights and went out. There was a car in the road a few yards away, its lights off.

"Probably just your imagination," he said when he came back. "There is a car, but there's no one in it." But he was not quite sure.

"I'm not going to worry." Poppy flung herself down on the sofa. "If Reed wants to find out what I'm doing, let him."

"What are you doing?"

"Working. I go to the Museum School every day to a life class. It's marvelous. Of course they're all kids, but they've been so kind, Phil!"

"Brandy?" As he poured carefully, he felt the impact of Poppy as more than he had bargained for—Poppy much too fat, relaxed, in some kind of smock, bright blue over pale green slacks. She reminded him of Harry—yes, there was the same contented-lion look, a look of lazy power, of being at home in the world. "You look like Harry all of a sudden . . . The twins were here for supper."

"They told me you had asked them. What an angel you are!"

"Quite the other way round. They were the first breath of fresh air I've had in weeks. We had a fine time. Harry is coming into his own—it's great to see that."

"Reed is so mean about the printing press. It was a terrific bargain and Harry had to make up his mind the day he found it, so I told him to go ahead. Reed is furious."

"Why didn't he ask Reed? He must have known what would happen."

"Reed was away, don't you remember? Reed was in Dallas on business."

"Oh, yes—let's not talk about him—I'm so glad to see you. You can't imagine! Can't we talk about you?"

And then, as though they were suspended in mid-air, a silence fell. Philip lifted his eyes and met Poppy's inquisitive, tender, probing look. And, drawn into her atmosphere, he didn't lower his eyes. But what he found there in hers was also panic.

"I'm going to lose you," she said calmly.

"Why do you say that? I don't believe I've ever been as glad to see you as I am right now."

"But you don't want the truth. You want to keep things in safe compartments. I'm in one and Reed is in another, and never the twain shall meet."

"Oh, Poppy, it's such a crucial time, that's all. After things get settled, we can talk again about everything."

"But now is when I need to talk!" And she added with an air of triumph, "You can't tell me that Reed and you never discuss me!"

"*Touché!*" Philip lit a cigarette, dismayed to see that his hand was shaking. "But Reed is so alone. You have your mother."

"He has his mother."

"He can't talk to his mother, Poppy. You know that!"

"No doubt she is playing the role of compassionate, all-understanding Kwan-yin. She would play it very well, as a matter of fact."

And they did not resist the burst of laughter this accurate vision brought on.

"What am I going to do with you, Poppy? You're irresistible. I had lunch with Cecilia—chiffon scarf, white gloves. But she is so grand! You must admit there is something grand about the way she handles a situation like this."

"By never facing the hard truth?"

"Oh, I think she tries to face it all, but in the process it gets transformed, however brutal, into something noble and heroic. She would find it easier to accept the divorce if you had fallen in love with someone else."

"Would she? How odd!"

"That would be a classic drama and her son's role would involve magnanimous self-sacrifice. The woman as artist she simply cannot take in."

"The woman as artist . . ." Poppy repeated. "Oh, I'm so frightened, Pip! I feel like someone who has jumped out of a plane and doesn't know whether the parachute will open!"

"But you felt like a prisoner in the plane . . . so . . ."

"Yes."

Philip was acutely aware of the pulse in Poppy's throat, of the fragility, the desperation there in the old friend, sitting as she had done for years on a sofa in this perfectly ordinary living room.

"I guess I'm really afraid of what people will think, of everyone waiting to see what will happen, whether I can make it. That's why I want to go far away—to Europe or Mexico, where no one knows anything about me."

"It might be lonely."

"I doubt it. You can hardly imagine how intoxicating I find it to sleep alone, not having to meet someone's expectations, passionate or otherwise, when all I want is to read in peace." And she turned on him her brilliant eyes. "You can't *know*, Phil!"

"But you're with Evelyn now. What will it be like when you are alone?"

Poppy sipped her brandy thoughtfully and set the glass down. "It will be better when I'm away from Evelyn."

"Why? She's certainly on your side."

"Don't you see, Pip, she's too much for me. She's a finished human being, in the sense of being complete. I'm a terribly unfinished, searching mass of conflict, doubt, rage. Mother is just too much for me at this point. I'm far more at ease with the kids at the Museum School." She settled back into the cushions comfortably. "Don't you think it's strange that Reed and I both have living parents? Most of our friends lost their parents ages ago. And as long as Reed's mother is alive, I have sometimes thought, he won't ever be able to become his real self."

"He doesn't pay much attention to her, does he?"

"Because he's involved in some frightful struggle between what she thinks he ought to be and what he really is."

"She has never appreciated the factory—that's for sure."

But Poppy had shifted her attention to Philip. He felt her eyes searching his face. "Do you miss your parents?"

"Yes, I guess I always will. They were so much more delightful and lovable than anyone else—my mother and my Aunt Agatha, I mean. You remember, she was a painter."

"You truly loved and admired them, didn't you? Reed doesn't love his mother. He's afraid of her."

Then she added, brushing that subject aside, "Tell me more about Aunt Agatha. She never married, did she? Was she a good painter?"

"I wonder . . . I think she did have a kind of genius for portraits, for getting the essence of a person, especially men, curiously enough. So she was immensely in demand and made piles of money. But whether she was a good painter in your sense of the word only time will tell. I think she was brilliant rather than deep. But she had a marvelous life, spent half the year in the south of France, often fell in love with her subjects as they did with her, and then forgot them . . ."

"How did she do that?"

"I've often wondered—she never confided in me, I was too young. Perhaps she could be deeply committed only to her art. She took that very seriously."

Poppy was listening intently and Philip basked in her attention. "For a small boy, she was simply the person who invented the best things in the world to do. Once she gave me a huge toy sailboat and we spent half a day sailing it in the Public Gardens and eating a picnic lunch on a bench. Sometimes she took me to the museum and plumped me down in front of a Chinese horse or something, gave me crayons and a sketching pad, and left me to draw for an hour. She loved theater and opera and took me with her often. When I was fourteen she had an opera cloak made to measure, dark blue with a white lining. Oh, she knew how to live!"

"And to spoil a small nephew!"

"She did give me expensive tastes, if that's what you mean."

"I was thinking that maybe she spoiled you for other women. You were a little in love with her, I suppose."

"Her smell of French vervain, her small very strong hands, her quick, bright eyes that took in everything—yes, I think she set a standard. Most girls seemed boring and stupid by comparison."

"I wish I'd known her!"

"But you mustn't think it was she who stood in the

way of my marrying—after all, she died when I was at St. Mark's."

"I wasn't thinking anything of the sort. How did you learn to be so understanding? You really love women, don't you, Pip? Few men do, I've decided."

"I don't know." Philip became shy before Poppy's passionate attention. "My mother may have had something to do with that." But he didn't want to talk about his mother. "By the time I met Reed at M.I.T. they were all dead . . . all dead in a few years. I felt cut off from everything. It was really a bad time for me all round."

"I shouldn't have thought Reed would be much comfort."

"Oh, but he was!"

"How? Tell me. I wish I could find the real Reed, at least in my mind. I don't like hating him. I don't like it at all. Hating Reed cancels out too much of my life. You do see that, don't you, Pip?"

"Reed . . ." Philip said the name, calling up the young man he first saw sculling on the Charles, coming in carrying his boat one day just as he himself was about to take his own out. "I don't know . . . I guess he challenged me. He pulled me out of physical sloth, you see, daring me to race him or jog two or three miles. He cut quite a dashing figure at that time, as you remember."

"He had exceptional vitality, one might say."

They exchanged a smile. How good to be able to talk about Reed without the anger!

"He did," Philip answered happily, "and that in itself is a kind of genius. Reed could work all night and play a fast game of tennis before breakfast. Beside him, I was lazy . . . and not really ambitious ever, as you have often told me, Poppy."

"Do you think it was bad that you inherited all that money?"

"It made life a lot easier than it might have been."

"It also made you a target—the most eligible bachelor in sight. Whatever happened to the girl you had then? What was her name?"

"Muriel? Emily?"

"Emily. That's it. When I first knew Reed, I thought you were engaged."

"Did you?" Philip was startled back into all that guilt. He didn't want to have to remember Emily. "Emily had a great sense of humor. We laughed till we cried, sometimes, but I could never have married her, Poppy, for God's sake!"

"Why not? What was wrong with Emily?"

"Nothing. I just didn't feel that way about her."

"And she suffered . . ."

"Oh, Poppy forget it. It's a long time ago and Emily is happily married and has six children." Philip couldn't bear to think of the girls, all the girls who had hoped to marry him. "But Reed . . ." He poured a small glass of brandy and held it up to the light. "I admired his brilliance, and he taught me a lot by asking questions. When it came to our work, I think we fed each other. We used to hash things out, use each other as sounding boards."

"Did you feel threatened when I came along?"

"Threatened? Why?"

"You might have minded . . ."

Philip was startled into laughter. "Poppy, when you came along, when you got married, I had a home again—it was wonderful!"

"We did have fun, didn't we?"

"Do you remember that leaky sailboat we rented? Oh, Lord!"

"And the trip to Revere when I got quite hysterical on the roller coaster?"

"It can't be over, Poppy!" The words jumped out before Philip thought what he was saying.

"Well, it is," she said, suddenly furious. The spell of the past, the few moments of respite were over. "Besides, it's not been like that for thirty years."

"You weren't married thirty years ago, you dunce."

"It feels like fifty." She was sitting upright now, her hands clasped, and she spoke with cold precision. "For the last ten years I've been sleeping with a man whom I do not respect. I doubt if that was good for Reed, and I know it was hell for me."

"What happened to Reed?"

"You're his best friend. Don't you know?"

Philip shook his head.

"I wish I did. I only saw symptoms. I can't diagnose the disease—though I have sometimes thought the disease was our society itself and its rotten values."

"Reed's temptation was success. Yet what's so bad about that? I never had his ambition."

"Maybe not. But you wanted to build houses that people could live their real lives in, didn't you? Sometimes you ruined a good design for people's sake. But people aren't included in Reed's calculations . . . that's one thing."

"His work isn't primarily concerned with people."

"But he employs two hundred of them. And he's a human being himself, isn't he? Pip, he closed himself in. The time came when I knew it was useless even to try to talk to him."

For a second Philip saw Poppy sitting there, so sure of herself, in a haze, very far away, as though he could not reach or touch her, and he needed so badly to tear through the haze, to bring her back into focus, to *see* her, that he shouted, "Maybe he tried and felt that it was useless . . . I mean, Poppy, you got so angry and screamed or cried. Reed felt battered."

"I had to scream because he didn't hear!"

"All I'm trying to say is there are two sides, Poppy."

Poppy put a hand over her eyes and murmured, "Don't let's fight, Pip. Please."

So he got up and went over and sat beside her, put an arm round her shoulders, and, as she turned toward him, they hugged each other silently. Then Philip broke away and sat there, his hands between his knees, slouched down. Would it ever end, the pulling and tearing?

After a long silence Poppy said, "Nobody really understands. Not even my mother."

"You've chosen a lonely path."

"But I had to . . . or die," she said quietly. Then she stood and walked up and down, stopping for a moment to look at the chrysanthemums. "You know about flowers. They have to have water."

"I don't know anything any more," Philip replied.

She stood, back to him, absent-mindedly rearranging the bunch as she talked. "It's hard, Pip, because everyone is trying to pin something on me. I have to be a great artist or there is no excuse for my behavior. But it's not that logical—how do I know whether I can do what I want? Our whole society demands *success.* If I divorce Reed there has to be a reason, and the reason can't be simply that I need the chance to grow. The reason can't be that I want to become a whole human being!"

"Well, you are enormously successful at one thing, my girl."

"What's that?"

"Making all of us around you aware of how we have compromised. I've taken a long hard look at myself these last weeks, I can tell you."

At this Poppy turned to him with a quick smile. "And what have you seen, Pip?"

"I suppose I've seen that like a cuckoo I made a comfortable home in another bird's nest. It's time I stopped borrowing."

"You do understand!" Poppy cried out, "You do understand, thank God!"

"Well," Philip laughed at her vehemence, "I don't know—"

"You see that we three were bound together all those years by our incompleteness. You completed our marriage. You provided what it lacked. And I suppose we supplied something you lacked—a home. Why did you never marry?"

"Too selfish, probably."

"No."

"You tell me."

Poppy gave him a queer little look, appraising, amused, and for a second he wondered whether

Reed had told her about Kathy. “Let’s leave it,” she said. When he got up she put her hands on his shoulders. “Thank you for letting me come.” Then she kissed him lightly on the mouth.

“I’ll walk you to your car.”

“Yes, we’ll scare off my follower if he’s still there.”

It was not a pleasant feeling to imagine that one might be observed. Instinctively Philip did not take Poppy’s arm, nor kiss her good-by after she was settled in the car.

“See you tomorrow at Reed’s,” she called. Philip stood and waved, as the headlights of the “follower’s” car came on, and the car turned out and sped away after Poppy’s white Dart.

Reed really is a little crazy, Philip thought. Did he still believe there was a lover?

Chapter XI

Five minutes before Poppy was due, Reed and Philip walked over to the studio together.

"I'm doing this against my lawyer's wish," Reed said. "He felt we shouldn't meet until the divorce was settled."

"What's happening today? What is this all about?" Poppy had not explained, Philip realized, and he had presumed that the initiative had come from Reed.

"Poppy's lawyer insisted that she must take nothing from the premises without my permission."

"Nothing? Not even her own clothes?"

"Oh, yes, she came and got them while I was at the factory one day last week. Lucy was here."

They had reached the door, and, after a second's hesitation, Reed opened it with his key. They entered a cold, empty room. In three weeks of neglect dust had accumulated. A mound of clay on the big table had dried and cracked. It felt like a tomb.

"Better get some heat going . . ." Reed went over to the big electric heater and turned it up to high.

The few pieces of sculpture standing around had been covered with grimy sheets; half the art magazines piled on a chair had slipped to the floor.

"Why don't you let Harry use the studio for his press?" The idea came to Philip out of the need to fill this vacuum that pulled desolation in like a fog.

"Not a bad idea," Reed answered rather surprisingly. "I had thought of renting it to an artist, could use the cash. I'll think it over."

It was on the tip of Philip's tongue to mention the detective on Poppy's tail. But just then they heard a car door slam, and Reed went out to the path and called, "We're at the studio! Come right along here."

Poppy took her time. They stood there, Reed in the doorway, Philip inside—one of those moments, Philip thought, when time stands still. What could she be doing? Looking at the garden? But when she swept past Reed in her black cape, and, without a word of greeting, went to the large figure she had been working on and tore off the sheet, her entire attention focused on that apparently, and stood there silently, Philip realized that he had been a fool to imagine he could manipulate the atmosphere of this meeting. Poppy would do that.

"Hello, Reed," she said after what seemed a very long minute.

"Well, I'm gratified that you recognize my presence!" Reed spoke quietly, but the edge in his voice was there, and Philip could not blame him for reacting in that way.

"Sorry, but I've been dying to see this thing . . . I thought about it all night."

"I quite understand. Your work, of course, must

come first now. People don't matter." This was exactly what Poppy had said of Reed a few hours ago and Philip couldn't help smiling. Reed caught the smile. "What in hell are you finding so amusing?"

"Nothing."

"Very well. Let's get down to business."

"It's freezing in here," Poppy said. "Would it be too much to ask for a sip of brandy?"

"I'll get it."

When Reed was out of hearing, Philip said, "Damn it, Poppy, I wish you hadn't asked me to do this. It's too miserable for words . . . this desolate cold place and Reed and you glaring at each other."

"Take it easy, Pip." For a second she laid a hand on his shoulder.

" 'She bid me take life easy, as the grass grows on the weirs . . .' "

" 'But I was young and foolish, and now am full of tears,' " Poppy shot back, just as she always used to do years and years ago. And, in spite of himself, Philip melted.

"Make this quick and businesslike, will you, Poppy? None of us can afford emotion at this point."

"That will be easy, because I feel none."

And then Reed was back again with brandy and glasses on a tray, and an ironic "At your service, madam," as he held it out for Poppy to pour herself a drink.

"Thanks." With the glass in her hand she pushed the remaining magazines off the chair and sat down. "Don't bother," she said to Philip, who was about to pick them up. "I'm through with all that."

Reed cleared his throat. "Will you send a mover to take whatever you need from here, or what?"

"I don't want anything."

"Not even the goose?" Philip was amazed. The marble goose had certainly been one of Poppy's successes. "May I have it, then?"

"Of course. I'm glad you think there is something worth salvaging out of this tomb," and she got up to uncover the goose, stroking it absent-mindedly, once it was revealed, in a wholly unself-conscious gesture that seemed to say that she did care more than she was going to admit.

Philip did not look at Reed, but he could feel the temperature rising.

"Everything here has been contaminated, you see." Reed's voice was high and strained.

"For heaven's sake, Reed, don't be dramatic! I expect to be traveling, and I can hardly carry a ton of not very important sculpture around with me, can I?"

"I'm going to need the studio. What do you want me to do with all this?"

"I have plenty of room in my cellar," Philip said, turning to Poppy. "Some day you might regret having thrown away ten years' work."

"I doubt it. I thought perhaps the big figure of a woman might be worth salvaging . . ." She looked again at the more than life-size piece about half finished, the chisel marks showing. "But it was, I now see, therapy, not art."

"You appear to see everything with quite extraordinary clarity," Reed said. "I envy you. I myself am in a total fog."

"Not my fault, dearie."

"I didn't say it was." Reed poured himself a brandy.

Philip watched him as one watches the fuse burning its way toward a rocket on the Fourth of July. Some outburst was inevitable, and really, he thought, might be less painful than the strain of the last few minutes. Then it came, blowing the silence and any attempt at the amenities sky-high. "God damn it, Poppy, I spent twenty thousand to build you a studio so you could do your *work*—and now you want to throw it all away . . . it's all *nothing!* I did it for *nothing!* That's pretty hard to swallow."

Philip caught Poppy's glance bidding him to take care of this, but unfortunately Reed caught it too.

"Let Poppy speak for herself, Phil." Then the second rocket went up. "I know you two are in each other's pockets, but my wife can speak for herself."

"Your detective must have a wild imagination. I've seen Pip twice in three weeks."

"What detective?" Reed asked blandly. "I don't know what you're talking about."

"You have someone trailing me," Poppy said, "I'm not so stupid as to be unaware of that. I resent it, Reed. Call your dogs off." So far she was as cold as ice, and that was a good thing, Philip thought.

"You're still my wife and you've run away from home. I have every right to find out what you are doing."

"It's such a waste of money," Poppy said gently. "What I'm doing is going to school and working hard. That's *all* I'm doing." There was no anger in her tone now, and Philip realized that she had spoken the truth when she said that she felt no emotion. Of course, that gave her the advantage, for Reed was visibly torn up, and longing, Philip suspected, for a fight, for something to end the frustration.

"People keep asking me where you are, Poppy . . ."

"And you tell them lies. Franny told mother that you had told Alan I was having a nervous breakdown. You've got to stop lying, Reed, for both our sakes."

"I'm not about to tell my friends that my wife, in her right mind, has walked out on me for *no reason*."

"I am not going to argue with you, Reed." Poppy half rose from the armchair, and for a second Philip wondered whether they might, after all, get out of this without a disaster. But in that second Reed had crossed the room and pushed Poppy roughly back into the chair.

"Don't touch me!"

Reed was standing, facing her, too close for anyone's comfort. "You're going to stay here a while longer, and you're going to tell me what this is all about."

Poppy refused to meet his eyes. "Philip, I want you to register that I am being forced to stay here against my will. And that I have just been rather roughly pushed."

"It's none of Phil's business. You're still my wife."

Philip was hot under the collar. He turned his back on them both, thinking that if he had any guts he would walk out. But he didn't have the guts, partly because he was afraid something awful might happen . . . he remembered Reed's saying that he might kill Poppy if they were left alone.

"Very well," he heard Poppy's crisp cold voice, "Philip is a witness." Then Reed's, furious again, "For God's sake, Poppy, try to tell me rationally what this is all about."

"I can't talk rationally to someone who shouts at me to be rational." Then she suddenly laughed.

Reed grabbed Philip and shook him. "She's laughing at me," he said in a strange high voice, and Philip saw that he was crying. The next thing he saw was Reed rushing at the big statue and with amazing force hurling it to the floor.

"Reed, for God's sake!"

"Let him do it." Poppy was fiercely cool. "He wants to kill me, of course . . . far better that he take it out on my work."

Reed, panting, his face red, sat down, clenching his fists. "Now, Poppy, please try to talk."

"It's not a very pleasant atmosphere you have created, Reed. I don't think I can."

"Oh . . ." Reed groaned. "I'm sorry. But I'm in pain, Poppy. You must understand that. I'm in pain." He put his head down in his hands.

Philip was crouched beside the fallen statue, trying to lift it. One arm had broken off.

"A man without anger couldn't possibly lift her," Poppy said. "It doesn't matter, Pip."

Exhausted, Philip stayed on the floor beside the broken marble. "Say something, Poppy. This is terrible."

There was a long silence. Philip heard Reed blowing his nose, heard Poppy strike a match. Finally he heard her say, "You're in this too, Pip."

"Of course he is. You two have always been in love—now you can admit it."

"Oh, Reed," she said sadly, "you couldn't be more wrong. Ten years ago there might have been some truth in that, not now."

"Who is it, then?"

"There has to be somebody, doesn't there? You can't believe that I'd have the guts to leave you without some protection. Well, I *have* the guts."

There was no doubt in Philip's mind that Poppy had changed. There she sat, large and flowing and somehow at peace. She had reached a place where the façade didn't matter any more. She was heavy; she was middle-aged; her hair was gray. It didn't matter.

"Please do talk to us, Poppy, if you have the words." Philip sat up, cross-legged. "It is quite necessary that you do."

For a moment she closed her eyes. When she opened them, she looked out the window. "I can speak only for myself. And I'll try, Reed." She turned to him as from a great distance. "If you'll let me say my say, and not interrupt."

"Very well." Reed stood, staring at her. Not easy, Philip thought, to endure that intense look, but Poppy seemed unaware of it, or pretended to be.

"It must have been about ten years ago . . . maybe less . . . that we began to die, all three of us. There was a change. For a long time I didn't understand what was happening, and I think—though this will seem preposterous to you, Reed—that it was the Watergate hearings that made me see it. All those young men—they might have been you and Pip twenty years ago—sensitive, ambitious, attractive, sure of themselves—persuasive—yet they were the damned. They had managed to allow the essential person to die, the conscience . . . I don't know how to define it, the absolutely private and singular judge we carry inside us. I suppose what I am trying to say is that they had, at some point, made a fatal compromise." Here Poppy, who had been looking out the window, turned toward Philip. "All three of us have done that to keep our relationship intact, so of course it began to wither. I'll begin with myself. I let Reed spend a lot of money on a studio so that I could *pretend* that it was possible to work seriously at an art and stay married to him . . . No, Reed," she said as Reed got up, "let me go on."

"I'm not interrupting," he answered pouring a small glass of brandy for himself.

"Ten years ago, Pip, you began to settle for habit and comfort—and for being the good friend you have been to us—at the expense of your own life. You stopped growing. I saw it happening. I was partly responsible. And Reed?" She paused and hesitated for the first time, but not, Philip thought, out of fear, simply to find the exact words. "You yourself must know, Reed, that you have compromised at the factory, and it began when you broke that strike."

"I know nothing of the kind . . . but I'll hold my peace till you're through."

There was nothing left of the old tentative Poppy. To Philip she seemed to have put herself at an infinite distance as she went on quietly, "Something went out of our marriage when my feelings about that were stifled, when you would not listen and pushed me off as ignorant and hysterical. You know very well what followed—the Vietnam war and your handling of Harry . . . forgive me, but I have to say it now . . . the terrible anxiety about him for two years, the whole dirty mess. I felt unclean. I was always getting sick. Pip then became a kind of nurse in a mental institution. We all three clung to the forms—Sunday dinner, a game of tennis. But what did we talk about? Do you remember how we used to argue years ago, how we listened to music, learned poems by heart?" Her voice had lost its cool and for the first time she looked at Reed, then Philip, as though trying to make some connection and not from way out there in outer space. "I guess I sound pretty didactic," she smiled. "But at least I'm clear in my own mind."

Philip had felt as she talked as though he were in an elevator sinking from the eightieth floor to the ground. The sensation of falling, as though he were in a dream, was so acute that it absorbed him completely. From far away he heard Reed talking in a stone-cold voice.

"You accuse me of lying, but it's you who have lied in a terrible way for years. You appeared to be willing enough to sleep with me."

"I was a coward. And sometimes sex broke the tension." Now she was looking straight at Reed and Philip felt that he did not exist, or should not be there. "Besides, I always hoped for a change, for an earthquake, for something that would rinse the eyes . . . I was, I see now, very naïve."

Reed laughed at that—a harsh laugh. "I'm the one who was naïve. Why didn't you say all this long ago?"

"I did!" This time Poppy, no longer cool, screamed the words in sudden fury. "I did—a thousand times and in every way I could. You never listened. You just pretended to listen, as though I were a fractious child, best ignored, punished, or cajoled. You never treated me as an equal, as a human being worthy of your real attention." And now, perhaps sensing Philip's embarrassed withdrawal, she turned to him. "You know that's true, Pip."

"Don't drag me into this, Poppy. It's between you and Reed." His own voice sounded strange to him. He was coming out of shock. For he began to see what had happened—all he had built up in himself of self-regard as a tender loving friend, one who could be counted on by both members of this marriage, had just been brushed aside, devalued, made into escape from life itself, a childish desire for shelter and comfort—had been failure. He saw that he had spent ten years trying to hold the marriage together, and that was a total illusion, for it had really been a cheap evasion of his own reality, a refuge from growth. Was this true?

"Well, Phil, you've been pretty well disposed of in the last few minutes by this lay psychoanalyst, haven't you?" Then Reed laughed exultantly and turned to Poppy. "I bet you don't know something I know about Phil, and that is that he's had a mistress for ten years! So there's *one* thing you read all wrong—Phil *didn't* stop growing ten years ago. He embarked on a secret life of his own!"

Philip was too numb by now even to care.

"Good," Poppy said coldly. "I'm glad to hear that. It doesn't change my view, however. It just means that Pip found a way to compartmentalize, to split himself up. Men are rather good at that. And it's one thing a woman can't do. When she does, she pays an enormous price." Then, as what Reed said got through to the inner person, she reacted with less self-assurance. "Why didn't you tell me about this person?" she asked Philip.

"Is this the time to talk about that?" he answered.

"Why not?" Reed shot back. "Here we are, the three of us, maybe for the last time. Why not get down to the nitty gritty once and for all?" This time he picked up the brandy bottle and refilled all three glasses.

"Language-wise," Poppy said with heavy irony, " 'nitty gritty' is a phrase that makes me sick."

"All right, give me a better one."

"The truth, forever adorable, even when hard to bear," Poppy said with such an air of assumed dignity, so unlike herself, that she caught it before the two men did, and laughed at the very instant Reed pounced.

"Divorce is making you into a pompous ass, my dear."

"Never mind." She was still smiling. "Please try to explain, Pip."

During this brief interchange Philip realized that, amazing as it seemed, these two were enjoying themselves. The painful confrontation had taken a new turn, and something of the atmosphere of their old bittersweet, furious arguments was being created now here in the abandoned studio, the broken marble statue at their feet. And he wondered, How can they separate? How *can* they?

"Get down to the adorable nitty gritty, Phil, for God's sake!" Reed said, lifting his glass.

"Why didn't I tell Poppy about Kathleen?"

"Kathleen?" Poppy raised her eyebrows.

"That's why. That tone. That air of faint amusement. Kathy is not exactly your kind of person. I didn't want to expose either of us." Philip quivered inwardly before what he was about to say, but there was nothing for it now but to come on strong. "Kathy is a detective. Now go ahead and laugh. It happens that she's a grand person and I love her."

But Poppy did not laugh. She was clearly upset. "Did you really think I was so inhuman, so class-bound or whatever you are suggesting, that I couldn't *understand?* Oh, Pip . . ."

"No, I was afraid of something getting hurt, something inside myself, too vulnerable . . . I was afraid not so much of what you might say as what you might *see*—about me, I mean." Philip turned away to look out at the leafless trees. "I suppose I wanted an unexamined natural happiness . . . and that is what I have had."

"Is that possible?" Poppy murmured.

"You've become rather cruel in your emancipation, Poppy. Are you aware of that?" Reed said.

"Cruel?" Poppy looked astonished. "I feel like a house that has been locked up for years and now all the doors and windows are open."

"It's not cruel to tell me our marriage was a locked house?" Reed bore down. "Come on, Poppy, you threaten us, Philip and me. You know you do. You threaten us," he said again as though realizing the full truth of what had just popped out of his mouth. "Yes, God damn it, you pretty well castrated Phil just now. That's why I told you about Kathy. Can't you see?"

"If Philip chose to have an affair with a woman he feels he can't marry, he's cut himself in two. You can't blame me for that. I had nothing to do with it."

"Oh, didn't you, though?" Reed put an arm round Philip's shoulders in mock affection, "She took the heart out of your body, didn't she, Philip? Didn't she?" he insisted.

Philip pulled away. "I can't imagine why you've become so jovial all of a sudden. But, to answer your question, no, she did *not!*" All the suppressed fury of the last weeks swept in and took Philip over. "You don't care, either of you, what's happened to me in the last three weeks, do you? You've tried to use me, each of you, in your power game against each other. You've expected me to talk to your mothers, your children. You've asked me to listen to your hatred and bitterness, to become a garbage can for all the filth. You didn't care what you were doing, but what you have been doing is destroying our friendship. You've made me feel, Poppy, that all you took from and gave to me was taken and given because I'm a cripple and you're a cripple and Reed's a cripple. Nothing is sacred. Everything has been torn down and made dirty."

"Except the truth, Pip."

"Where do we go from here? What is there to trust or believe in or love now?" Philip was shouting, but shouting brought no relief. Seeing the bottle standing on the workbench, he seized it and flung it through the window. There was a queer little sound of broken glass tinkling down. Then silence.

"Maybe we'd just better tear the whole place down while we're at it!" Reed said.

"Oh, no, we don't." Poppy heaved herself up from the low chair. "I'm getting out of here. Have you gone mad, Pip?"

"No." Philip was breathing heavily. He faced the

broken window, his back to Reed. "No," he said, licking his finger, which was bleeding. "I've gone sane. Sorry about the broken window. I'll see that it gets fixed."

"But, Pip . . ." Poppy was weeping. Philip could hear her caught breath.

"Yes, I know." Philip turned to face her. "No, don't touch me." For she had put out a hand as though to take his arm.

"All right, but please listen." Poppy blew her nose.

Philip wound a handkerchief round his finger carefully and slowly. He felt calm now and very, very remote. In fact, he was trying to remember what jobs he had on hand and when he could leave for Europe. He had decided to go away.

"Reed and I have been pigs. I see that now. You were right to hurl that bottle through the window."

"Hey," Reed said, "speak for yourself, Poppy."

"Will nothing ever make you look at yourself, Reed—not even what you have just heard?"

Philip groaned.

"I see perfectly well that Philip can't remain swung between the two of us, not taking sides," Reed said.

Philip looked straight at him. "If you think I'm going to take sides, you're dead wrong. And if you think I'm going to go on protecting you from whatever it is you have got to see, you're dead wrong too. I'm through with being a psychiatric nurse."

"Right on!" Poppy raised one arm in a half-humorous dramatic gesture, then stopped, narrowed her eyes, and murmured something. Then, "Yes, that's it!" she said in triumph. "I've got it at last.

Bogan! Remember? 'Time for the pretty clay,/ Time for the straw, the wood./ The playthings of the young/ Get broken in the play,/ Get broken, as they should.' "

"So where are we now?" Philip asked.

"In limbo between the fallen marble statue and the broken glass."

"We're not children. We're middle-aged," Reed said.

"Middle-aged children are the very worst," Poppy said. "Don't you honestly see that we may all three have to grow up?"

"Couldn't we try to do it together, Poppy?" Reed asked gently and gravely, and Philip knew that that question was an enormous capitulation. It was followed by silence.

Then Poppy did an odd thing. She picked up the heavy marble goose, a round, restful object, head folded under its wing, and held it in her arms as though it were a child, something vulnerable that must be protected, something that also, like a child, protected her. There was no anger in the gesture, only something, Philip thought, inconsolable. He was touched. Poppy—middle-aged as a physical presence, and yet poignantly and truly young as a nonmaterial presence—held their complete attention.

"No," she said then. She handed the goose to Philip. "I'm glad the goose will stay with you. I think it's not bad."

But this moment of reconciliation, Philip knew, as he set the goose down on the table, had nothing to do with Poppy and Reed.

"It's your last chance," Reed said very quietly.

"And if you don't take it, if you won't even try to mend all you have broken . . ."

"*I* have broken?" Poppy, who had interrupted him, was not allowed to go on.

"Shut up, and listen to me! If you stick to your childish decision to walk out on twenty-seven years of marriage, if you, a living human being, choose to walk out for the sake of a marble woman—for that's what it amounts to, isn't it?—I'm going to fight you with all I've got. And that means that your dream of glory, of studying in Europe and all that, is going to depend on your *earning* it. Since the children are not involved, the settlement will be minimal."

"Your lawyer is a Roman Catholic, I hear," Poppy said.

"Yes, he is. Anything wrong with that?"

"No." She pushed her hair back with an impatient gesture. "It only shows that, even when it comes to this, you are willing to compromise to get what you want. You are using another man's religion to back you up. You have deliberately chosen a male chauvinist, buttressed by rigid church dogma in which you don't believe, to do your dirty work. Do you think I want your money?"

"No settlement at all?" Reed grinned. "That can easily be arranged."

Philip had listened to this savage interchange, not even trying to intervene. Now he said lightly, "You have to admit we are now *en plein* nitty gritty!"

"You can't help, Philip. Don't try," Poppy said shortly. Then she turned to Reed. "Have you ever wanted to do anything for its own sake, Reed? I mean, even the games you play are competitive . . .

tennis. Have we ever gone for a walk for no purpose except to look at the autumn leaves? I can't accept your offer to try again . . . to grow up together . . . because you'll never believe in me as an artist unless I win a prize or have a show. You'll never, never in this world understand what I felt when I was hammering that goose out of a piece of marble—the fierce struggle it was, the joy it was. My competition is with *myself,* you see. Yours is with the world." Philip watched her mood change from self-assurance to self-doubt and anguish. "Oh, Reed, will you ever understand anything? Always with you I feel I am screaming in a high wind to someone who can't hear . . . It's horrible." Tears flowed down her cheeks, though she seemed not to notice them.

"May I say something now?" Philip asked.

"We're beyond help, Pip."

"You're very different people. Why is that fact unacceptable? Why isn't it possible to accept differences?"

"Because people either grow together or they die together. Don't you *see?*"

"I'm not dead yet," Reed said irritably. "Damn it, where's that bottle of brandy? Do you think I don't get a fierce joy out of *my* work? You don't care. You've never listened when I tried to tell you what we were developing—at the moment a little gadget that might make electric cars possible." He looked across at Poppy, found no response, and shrugged his shoulders. "Oh, well . . . it's hopeless."

But Philip had had time to think and he had things to say now. "We've been brought up, I suppose, to believe that things don't change. One makes a commitment and it has to be forever. But I think Poppy has faced something you and I haven't faced."

"And what is that, Rosencrantz?"

"Well, I guess I have to admit that whatever has been happening in this country for the last ten years *has* affected every one of us, has eaten into us, has somehow undermined faith in anything and everything. It's like slime, all the lying and corruption. I can understand the fever one might go through trying to get clean, to make a fresh start, to find firmer ground to stand on. Poppy has really been going through a religious conversion."

"Not religious, I'm afraid," Poppy murmured. "I'm just fighting for my life."

"All right, then I'm fighting for mine," Reed said. "You're part of my life, Poppy. The house has become a tomb. The garden is a morgue. Everything is dying around me."

Philip wondered whether mention of the garden, the one thing they had created together except for the children, would melt Poppy. Perhaps she was moved by this plea, for she said quickly, "I've got to go now."

She moved around the big table toward the door, but Reed blocked her way.

"Oh, no, you don't," he said. "We're going to have this thing out once and for all—NOW."

"We've had it out. Don't be childish." She pushed him roughly, but Reed reacted instantly, pinning her arms to her sides.

"Let me go! Philip!"

But Philip's ability to respond actively had been spent with the sound, long ago, of broken glass. He waited for whatever was to happen with something like indifference. What happened was that Poppy, unable to get free, capitulated.

"Let me go. I'll listen."

Reed brushed the sweat out of his eyes. He was breathing heavily. Poppy had gone back to her chair and sat there in stubborn silence. "How can I say it now?" Reed murmured.

"I don't think you can," Philip said. He knew the use of force had been fatal. "You'd better leave it to the lawyers, Reed."

"What do the lawyers know about my marriage?" Reed said, anguish in his voice.

"You seem to have persuaded your lawyer, at least, that it was a dismal affair with a half-*mad* woman!" Poppy said tonelessly. "Please let me go now, Reed."

"Couldn't you wait six months, Poppy? Couldn't you wait and see?"

It was excruciating for Philip to watch Reed crumble, the anger spent and only naked need showing at last.

"But that would be only another compromise. I'm through with compromises," she said in the same dull tone. "It's too late, Reed."

Reed took a deep breath. "Very well. Then let's at least part friends."

"How can we? If we could *part* friends, we could *stay together* as friends, can't you see?"

Reed opened the door and stood aside. Very slowly Poppy picked up her purse from the floor and got to her feet. She moved, Philip thought, as though she were swimming under water, with difficulty, and after what seemed a very long while Reed followed her down the path, and Philip closed the door to the studio and stood there, outside, until he heard her car tires grinding the gravel, and she was gone. Now he had to decide what to do. To abandon Reed at this moment seemed impossible, and to stay, equally impossible. He looked up at the sky which had darkened in the hour they had spent inside.

"It looks like rain," he said as Reed started back toward him. "I'd better get along. Left the door open onto the terrace. There might be a storm."

The End